The Charismatic Leader

Jay A. Conger

THE
CHARISMATIC
LEADER

Behind the Mystique of
Exceptional Leadership

Jossey-Bass Publishers

San Francisco • Oxford • 1991

THE CHARISMATIC LEADER
Behind the Mystique of Exceptional Leadership
by Jay A. Conger

Copyright © 1989 by: Jossey-Bass Inc., Publishers
350 Sansome Street
San Francisco, California 94104
&
Jossey-Bass Limited
Headington Hill Hall
Oxford OX3 0BW

Library of Congress Cataloging-in-Publication Data

Conger, Jay Alden.
    The charismatic leader : behind the mystique of exceptional
leadership / Jay A. Conger. — 1st ed.
        p.   cm. — (The Jossey-Bass management series)
Bibliography: p.
Includes index.
ISBN 1-55542-171-7 (alk. paper)
    1. Leadership. 2. Charisma (Personality trait) I. Title.
II. Series.
HD57.7.C66   1989   89-45598
658.4'092—dc20   CIP

Manufactured in the United States of America

The paper in this book meets the guidelines for
permanence and durability of the Committee on
Production Guidelines for Book Longevity of the
Council on Library Resources.

JACKET DESIGN BY WILLI BAUM

FIRST EDITION
    First printing: July 1989
    Second printing: May 1991

Code 8945

The Jossey-Bass
Management Series

Consulting Editors
Organizations and Management

Warren Bennis
University of Southern California

Richard O. Mason
Southern Methodist University

Ian I. Mitroff
University of Southern California

To Lianne and Clem,
Bill and Shelley

CONTENTS

ix

PREFACE

Most of us have known leaders at work, in the community, in government, who capture our imagination with a passion for an idea—a vision of the way the future could be. When they speak, we find ourselves mesmerized by their words and drawn by their sense of urgency. They seem to possess a certain indescribable energy that inspires and motivates. They appear to touch our emotions more than our rational mind. Things happen when they are around. There is change. And often we find ourselves, quite willingly, drawn to them. We may also find ourselves performing beyond our expectations to accomplish their goals. Most of all, we are moved by them—and, quite frequently, moved to follow them.

What is at the core of their power? *Charisma* is one word that comes to mind. Yet if asked to describe what we mean by their charisma, most of us would stumble in thought for a moment. We may summarize in a phrase or two what we mean, but somehow our explanation does not really capture this elusive quality. Even social scientists who have spent decades unraveling the mysteries of leadership have fallen short of an adequate description. Why certain people come to be perceived as charismatic leaders eludes us.

As I hope to show, however, charisma and charismatic

leadership need not remain a mystery forever. In these pages I hope to strip away some of their mystique. Drawing on important new research, I will explain the forces responsible for this elusive quality. Not only have these projects expanded our understanding of this potent form of leadership but, as well, these new discoveries indicate that charismatic leadership can teach us much about entrepreneurship, the management of change, strategic vision, motivation, and other vital areas of management. Because of the many important lessons these leaders have to teach us, I have written this book with a broad audience in mind. Executives, managers, organizational development consultants, management training specialists, professors, students—in short, anyone interested in the subject of leadership—should find this book full of valuable insights.

A Neglected Subject of Study

Charismatic leaders have been largely ignored as a subject of serious study. There are several reasons for this neglect. First, the term *charisma* itself is ambiguous. You and I may apply the same word to describe someone with a charming personality in one moment and in the next to explain the inspirational powers of John F. Kennedy. Even U.S. President Lyndon Johnson would complain that his trouble was that he lacked charisma. (He pronounced it with a soft "ch") (Burns, 1978, p. 244). It is a term that in the public's mind encompasses a broad range of human qualities. At the same time, we find the task of describing the source of one's charisma a baffling experience. Like the general public, academics too ascribe a sense of mystery to charisma. They have assumed that something so elusive is methodologically too difficult to study. Moreover, charismatic leaders, especially in business, were until recently thought to be rare and isolated cases. They were so unusual and their qualities so elusive that there was little reason to study them.

Neglect of the topic might have continued if it were not for several forces that recently conspired to bring our attention to this subject. The first was the tremendous change in the competitive environment of North American industry. Throughout the 1970s and 1980s, organizations that had grown huge and bureaucratic were suddenly faced with pressures to innovate and change their ways. Instead, many stumbled. Their market shares eroded and layoffs became commonplace. In response to these problems, the experts began to search for solutions. A wave of books appeared proclaiming the virtues of competitive strategy making, of entrepreneurship, of quality of work life, of corporate culture, of transformational leadership, of worker participation. A search was under way for new ideas, for new management processes, that could aid in the transition to a more competitive environment. A major focus of this search was the role of leadership. A surprising number of books appeared on the subject. Their argument was simple: More effective leadership was needed to revitalize North American industry. (See, for example, Bass, 1985; Bennis and Nanus, 1985; Kotter, 1988; Lamb, 1987; Tichy and Devanna, 1986.)

The second catalyst was the appearance of corporate turnaround artist Lee Iacocca of Chrysler and entrepreneurs like Steven Jobs of Apple Computer. These men and their stories seemed to capture the imagination of a public yearning for signs of America's vitality. Their swashbuckling charm and risk-taking heroism were appealing. They became the business heroes of the 1980s. They were also a breed of business leader distinctly different from earlier times. Unlike the Henry Fords, William Vanderbilts, or John D. Rockefellers who were portrayed as tough industry barons with visions of personal aggrandizement, this new breed of leader spoke about contributions to society, about revitalizing industry, about creating meaningful products and services. They were able to inspire and motivate on a grand scale. Often they were gifted speakers. And unlike those who preceded them, they were skilled in marketing—especially in marketing themselves. Soon the word *charismatic* began to appear beside their names. For the first time, business leaders began to share the limelight with great political leaders. With the publicity and attention they received, the notion that charismatic leaders could be found in the corporate world began to take root.

Thus interest in leadership has been growing—especially among management researchers. Although the new publicity is a revival of research interests begun decades before, it is of a profoundly different nature. Beginning in the 1970s and gaining momentum throughout the 1980s, there has been a growing disenchantment with yesterday's focus on what we today call "managership." Researchers at the time were curious about the extent to which managers were task-oriented or people-oriented and the degree to which they involved others in their decisions. Management theorists like Henry Mintzberg (1973, 1982) argued that such research had failed to distinguish between leadership and managership. Too much research, he argued, dealt with day-to-day supervisory or managerial roles instead of the leader's influence on strategic direction and organizational change. As a result, interest in the leader as a source of strategic vision and an agent of innovation grew. (See Bass, 1985; Bennis and Nanus, 1985; Tichy and Devanna, 1986.) Attention moved up the organizational pyramid to focus on executive positions rather than simply on first-level supervisors on the factory floor. (See, for example, Kotter, 1982; Levinson and Rosenthal, 1984.)

As an outcome of these forces, an interest in charismatic leadership has emerged. Intrigued by its links to innovation and change, social scientists like myself have begun exploring this elusive phenomenon. We are striving to understand the qualities that create perceptions of charisma as well as the lessons it may hold for effective leadership. And though our studies are still quite exploratory, a growing body of knowledge is giving shape to what has been an almost mystical subject.

The Aim of This Book

Part of the drive to understand charismatic leaders is based on a sense that they hold certain keys to transformational processes within organizations and, for that matter, entire industries and societies. Certainly there are perceptible differences between the impact of a charismatic leader and a noncharismatic leader. In the companies where I have studied leadership, I have seen remarkable differences in the levels of creativity, motivation, commitment, and even the personal zeal that the subordinates of charismatic leaders bring to their work. As I will describe, however, not all of these differences are positive.

My purpose in undertaking this book is to penetrate the mystery of charisma and help us see its shape and form. More precisely, I hope to accomplish the following objectives:

- To outline the behavior that appears to distinguish charismatic leaders from others
- To discover how this constellation of behavior, when taken together, creates the perception of charisma and influences followers and organizations
- To illuminate the role of charismatic leaders in organizational change and innovation
- To examine the harmful effects these leaders can have on organizations
- To suggest how managers and organizations might employ these leaders or develop certain of their qualities to increase organizational effectiveness

This is an ambitious and perhaps audacious undertaking since our answers to these points are still evolving. The reader must bear in mind, therefore, that much of this discussion is still speculative. My intention is to show how complex the phenomenon actually is and to emphasize the value of charismatic leadership for organizational effectiveness.

Sources of Data

Much of the conceptual foundation of this volume is drawn from a study I conducted during 1984–1985 and from biographical studies and other research since that time. My initial research was designed to compare a group of business executives described as charismatic with other business executives described as noncharismatic. To avoid confounding effectiveness with charisma, I chose only effective leaders. For information on methodology, see the Resource section at the end of the book.

Essentially the project was an exploratory study designed to establish hypotheses for later testing; as such, its conclusions are tentative. This research provided the behavioral components of charismatic leaders described in this volume. The concepts based on these findings were further refined through work with my colleague Rabindra Kanungo. The product of our collaboration (see, for example, Conger and Kanungo, 1987, 1988a) constitutes an important basis for this book.

Each behavioral dimension is also supported by the literature—for example, qualities such as vision, articulation skills, empowerment, and unconventionality and risk taking have been reported in other studies. (See, for instance, Bass, 1985; Bennis and Nanus, 1985; House, 1985; Martin and Siehl, 1983; Roberts, 1984; Willner, 1984; Zaleznik and Kets de Vries, 1975.) As well, many of the behavioral outcomes among followers have been tested by Avolio and Bass (1985), Bass (1985), Conger and Kanungo (1988b, 1988c), House (1985), Howell (1985), Smith (1982), and Yukl and Van Fleet (1982). Although I comment throughout the text on the areas where researchers are in agreement and where they are not, readers wishing greater depth should consult Conger (1988) and Conger and Kanungo (1988d).

What is unique about the material presented here is its systematic approach to how these behavioral components work together to create the perception of charisma. With the exception of my work with Kanungo, earlier studies have generally failed to show the complex interrelationship between the leader's behavior and the followers' perceptions of his or her charisma. As well, this volume explores more deeply such issues as the liabilities of charismatic leaders, the formulation of vision and its effective articulation, and the implications of charismatic leadership for organizations—issues where research to date has only scratched the surface.

Apart from the body of research just described, I have also drawn upon biographical materials about charismatic business leaders to illustrate the points I make. I have searched for articles and books on executives who have been described as charismatic leaders—such figures as Donald Burr of People Express, Jan Carlzon of Scandinavian Airlines, John DeLorean of General Motors, Dee Hock of Visa International, Lee Iacocca of Chrysler, Steven Jobs of Apple Computer, Mary Kay Ash of Mary Kay Cosmetics, Edwin Land of Polaroid, Bob Lipp of Chemical Bank, Don Massaro of Xerox, Archie McGill of American Telephone and Telegraph, Ross Perot of Electronic Data Systems, and Fred Smith of Federal Express.

My purpose in using this material is twofold. First, my research and that of others has focused on short-term or static studies of leaders. There is little longitudinal or historical material on charismatic leaders. To understand any form of leadership, though, it is imperative that we look at it over the long run. Biographical material allows us to do exactly this. Secondly, I have found that biographical materials, especially if collected from several sources, can lend a certain richness of detail that is difficult to obtain simply through clinical field studies. For these reasons, I have chosen to illustrate my points extensively with anecdotal material from biographical sources.

While there are certain problems inherent in biographical and journalistic material such as the need for a "good story," or the distortion of certain events, or retrospective hindsight, I have chosen material on the same leader from a variety of authors and through cross-checking have attempted to minimize distortion and bias. I have also searched for material that presented both the positive and the negative faces of the executive. Finally, I have selected material that captures the leader at different points in time from multiple perspectives providing important longitudinal and objective information.

In addition to these sources of data, I have also drawn upon an extensive and diverse body of research in the social sciences to illuminate charismatic leadership at its deeper and more complex levels. Wherever possible, material is supported by research in management studies, psychology, sociology, and political science. It is not enough to determine which behavior leads to the perception of charisma—we must also understand *why* it does. The behavioral sciences are helpful in this respect.

Overview of the Contents

I begin the book by exploring in Chapter One the basic reasons why we need to understand charismatic leadership. Here we examine the case history of one highly successful charismatic leader who ultimately appears to have failed at the peak of his career. His history highlights many of the possibilities—and liabilities—associated with charismatic leadership. His story sets the stage for the rest of the book. As we uncover the components of his charisma, we are able to see the power of these leaders and to understand its composition. This case study highlights important implications for the development, training, and management of charismatic leaders—issues I discuss in later chapters. In Chapter One I also expand upon the reasons why charismatic leadership is so important for today's organizations and highlight the many areas in which charismatic leaders may have a profound influence—for these leaders and their unique skills are essential in managing large-scale change in our organizations today.

In Chapter Two, I begin outlining the basic dimensions that distinguish charismatic leaders from noncharismatic ones. As well, we will explore the psychological reasons why you and I attribute charisma to one leader and not to others.

With Chapter Three, we begin an in-depth examination of the individual components that make up a leader's charisma. We start with strategic vision. Using case histories, we can trace the general process of "visioning."

Chapter Four looks at a related issue—the art of communicating the vision. In many ways, communication skills are just as important as the content of the vision itself. Here we will examine how charismatic leaders communicate their organizational goals so powerfully.

Chapter Five analyzes the manner in which charismatic leaders build trust and commitment to themselves and their vision. Rather than using coercion or other means, these leaders skillfully build exceptional trust in their seemingly impossible goals. In Chapter Five we will discover just how they do this.

Chapter Six looks at the way in which charismatic leaders motivate subordinates and how they demonstrate the pathways to success for their organizations. Their unique approach involves a process called empowerment that makes subordinates feel more self-assured and open to risk. As a result, productivity under these leaders often appears to be extraordinary.

In Chapter Seven, we turn to the question of followership. Charismatic leaders are popularly believed to be potent mesmerists. Indeed, their followers often go to extremes of loyalty and effort for their leader. The dynamics of this powerful bond are explored in this chapter.

Chapter Eight directs our attention to a crucial issue—the liabilities of charismatic leaders. While these figures are renowned for their positive impact on the world, some have a history of questionable outcomes. As well, certain elements of their leadership style may be problematic for organizations. In Chapter Nine I conclude with a look at what organizations can do to develop the qualities associated with charismatic leaders as well as the implications for managing them.

Acknowledgments

The subject of charismatic leadership has a long history of interest for me. Without being too Freudian, I can trace the first spark of curiosity to my childhood. My parents had a great interest in politics and political leaders, and the dinner table always provided a forum for great debates. I owe my parents a debt of gratitude for encouraging me to become involved in issues of leadership. Their support led to personal involvement in politics and ultimately to the important question of why one leader could be so much more effective than another in gaining popular support and implementing change.

More recently, several mentors have played a vital role in encouraging me to explore this topic: Jack Gabarro, John Kotter, and Vijay Sathe were my advisers as a doctoral student at the Harvard Business School. For a graduate student, a topic such as charismatic leadership is considered a high-risk undertaking—in fact, many would consider it a foolhardy undertaking. These men nonetheless had the conviction that somehow I might discover important insights. Their support was invaluable. They taught me that achievement involves taking risks.

Another person who has played a particularly important role in deepening my understanding of charismatic leadership has been my colleague at McGill University, Rabindra Kanungo. Through our mutual explorations and debates, Rabi has played a major part in my own understanding of leadership. I am greatly indebted to him. This book is in part a reflection of our joint explorations. I would also like to acknowledge several people who reviewed early drafts of this volume: Warren Bennis, Lee Bolman, Ann Feyerhen, Ian Mitroff, Charles and Dale Scarlett, and Edgar Schein. Their comments were especially valuable. Finally, the typing of the various drafts was done by Jean Hepworth, whose cheerfulness and constant prodding kept me in good spirits and on schedule.

Montreal, Quebec   Jay A. Conger
January 1989

THE AUTHOR

Jay A. Conger is assistant professor of organizational behavior at the Faculty of Management, McGill University, Montreal. He received his B.A. degree in anthropology, with honors (1974) from Dartmouth College, his M.B.A. degree (1977) from the University of Virginia, and, after a stint as an international marketing manager, his D.B.A. degree (1985) from the Harvard University Graduate School of Business Administration.

Conger's research centers on charisma, executive leadership, the management of change, and the training and development of leaders. He is particularly interested in the role that leaders play in revitalizing troubled organizations and in entrepreneurial leadership. His work on these subjects has been published in numerous articles and papers. His most recent book is *Charismatic Leadership: The Elusive Factor in Organizational Effectiveness* (1987, coedited with Rabindra N. Kanungo). He is also an active consultant to many major corporations in the United States and Canada.

The Charismatic Leader

Chapter 1

Two Faces of the Charismatic Leader

In the early 1970s, American Telephone and Telegraph (AT&T) hired a brash and visionary figure named Archie J. McGill to serve as its director of marketing. The move was unprecedented for the company: Never before had AT&T hired an outsider for such a high-level executive position.

But it was an unprecedented move for unprecedented times. AT&T was leaving the comfort of its monopoly and its stable marketplaces. Less than a decade later, it would lose its operating companies. It had been forewarned by a consulting company in 1972 that it had no means of addressing customer needs effectively. Even at that time, its equipment markets were being flooded by the products of competitors from all over the world. In some cases, its market share had simply withered. To avert a potential crisis, the company turned to the outside. Archie McGill seemed like the right choice. A marketing man, he was at age thirty-three the youngest vice-president at IBM ever. He was full of energy, charisma, and ambition. He believed in action: To him, a fast response to the market was more important than internal efficiencies. As he used to say, "I'd rather swing at a bad pitch to get on base than let a thousand balls

1

pass, waiting for the perfect one." His philosophy was in stark contrast to the conservative culture at AT&T.

McGill is best described as restless—a characteristic typical of many charismatics. His interests were always with the future. "Nostalgia doesn't generate sales. I have a healthy respect for the Bell heritage, but I also have a healthy respect for what the future requires of us," he would say (Wilbins, 1982, p. 14). His revolutionary spirit would bring change to AT&T. It would also bring problems.

Joining AT&T in 1975 as director of marketing, McGill quickly rose to become president of the company's new business communications division by the early 1980s. Within a decade, he would go from managing thirty or forty people to managing eighteen thousand individuals. Along the way, he professionalized the company's sales force, helped restructure the organization to make it more competitive, introduced extensive market research programs, and in general turned AT&T marketing into a significant function of the company. He also recruited many talented co-workers from his former employer, International Business Machines, and from such highly respected consumer-oriented companies as Proctor and Gamble.

A large part of his success was tied to his leadership style. He was a demanding leader who motivated, prodded, and intimidated subordinates into action. He built a highly cohesive and highly driven team. His charisma inspired and excited others. As one executive described the experience, "People were charged up . . . the field identified so strongly with McGill. He was an advocate of sales, of working with the customer, and of greater professionalism. He was a champion of aggressive marketing." The end result was a highly visible salesman for the company and a transformation in the nature of marketing at AT&T. "McGill is the most recognizable name in American Bell," remarked Gus V. Morck, Atlantic Richfield's manager of corporate electronics and telecommunications to *Business Week* ("AT&T's Supersalesman . . . ," 1983).

But then, surprisingly, something went wrong. On June 7, 1983, company officials announced that the man whom some described as singlehandedly revitalizing the competitive spirit at

American Telephone and Telegraph had handed in his resignation. Archie J. McGill was stepping down from the company he had helped to transform.

The communications industry was in shock. "It can't do anything but retard their move into competitive markets," declared H. Michael Doran, president of Teltone Corporation, a communications equipment manufacturer. Robert Casale, the man who inherited many of McGill's responsibilities, "is not the same legendary and luminary leader [as McGill]," commented James R. Carreker, vice-president of the market research firm Dataquest. *Business Week* noted that "the shuffle is certain to create confusion among customers and employees" ("AT&T's Supersalesman . . . ," 1983).

This might have been an ordinary resignation if it were not for the fact that McGill had done so much for AT&T. Here was a man who had helped invigorate one of America's largest corporations, and now he was suddenly departing. What had gone wrong?

According to company officials, McGill had volunteered to leave. AT&T was dividing his position as president of Advanced Information Systems, the company's business systems division, into the responsibilities of two operating units. According to company officials, the aim was to streamline American Bell to concentrate more effectively on sales to business customers. As a result, the reorganization of the deregulated AT&T left McGill with responsibilities overlapping those of American Bell's chairman, Charles Marshall. Marshall explained, "Arch and I found ourselves one-on-one, so we began looking at how best to reassign and use our people." During the discussion, "Arch thought this was the time to move," Marshall recalled. McGill agreed: "We discussed alternatives, but what I set out to do has been accomplished, so I think it's time to move on" ("AT&T's Supersalesman . . . ," 1983).

Sources close to the situation said that McGill had been offered a new presidential position within another division, Western Electric. The dilemma, however, was that the offer meant shifting from the highly visible, flagship position of the company to a behind-the-scenes job with a small staff. In essence, the new position could only be perceived as a step down. McGill would later argue in an interview that he had already made his decision to leave AT&T some two months earlier. It was only a question of when. The reorganization provided a suitable opportunity to exit ("AT&T Unit's McGill Resigns . . . ," 1983, p. 26).

I suspect, however, that these answers reflect more the nature of public relations than the inside story of why McGill was leaving. Though we may never know the complete answer, I believe that McGill's departure had a great deal to do with the power of charisma and its liabilities. Let me explain what I mean.

Profile of a Charismatic Leader

Charismatic leaders are by vocation change agents. They see the shortcomings of any situation. McGill would often say, "I have an intolerance for 'what is' and for 'what has been.' I believe everything can be done better. People are never contributing to the best of their abilities. There are always new opportunities, always ways to contribute more."

This sense of dissatisfaction with the status quo is a restless energy within the charismatic leader. Such leaders seem forever discontent and in search of new opportunities. They are entrepreneurs whether they are the head of their own company or a member of a large corporation. They are also impatient—things have to change and today. "I don't need to think too long before I make a decision. If I see a need for action, I act," McGill often remarked (Wilbins, 1982). One manager describing his charismatic boss told me: "He's impulsive about change. He's always looking for new opportunities and even new ways of doing old things. It seems like he's on a constant search for a bigger challenge." This is the mentality of a charismatic leader.

As a result, things do happen more quickly. Impatience translates into action. McGill's drive transformed marketing at AT&T in a relatively short period of time, just as Steven Jobs and Dr. Edwin Land were able to develop and launch successful versions of the personal computer and the instant camera faster than others. But a price must be paid for such impatience. In large organizations, the charismatic's intolerance for the status quo may alienate others. "Arch grated on people," commented Harry Newton, a telecommunications consultant. "He's a rebel who's not averse to letting others know that he's a rebel. He deliberately fosters an image of being a shaker," said an ex-colleague. Before AT&T, McGill's colleagues at IBM had noted that his intolerance for IBM's bureaucracy was wearing thin when he departed from the company. "He couldn't deal with it," remarked Carl Vorder Bruegge, a senior vice-president at MCI in a 1982 interview. "I'm surprised he can stand it at AT&T" (Gay, 1982, p. A8). This impatience with the status quo led McGill to challenge the systems and management of AT&T directly. In his race to change the company, McGill was sowing the seeds of antagonism. The advantage of the charismatic leader—impatience with the status quo—can also become a liability.

Another quality of charismatics, tied to their sense of opportunism, is an ability to resolve shortcomings and motivate change through a strategic vision. This vision becomes a beacon for subordinates and indeed for an organization searching to adapt in an uncertain world. It provides a certain clarity at a time when things may not be very clear.

McGill, for example, astutely recognized that many of the key innovations in telephone technology would come from systems operating within a user's offices instead of their traditional source—the telephone company's own network. This understanding, according to subordinates, provided direction and encouraged their commitment to his ideas: "Arch's a very easy guy to follow, especially with his track record. He would see an announcement, say it was significant, and predict what would happen with relative accuracy. For instance, in 1975, he saw a need to integrate [telephone] technology on the user's premises. Many people, on the other hand, were arguing that the [telephone company's] network was the battleground, not the offices. . . . He's been right on the technology, the markets, and so on. He's been able to predict with a vision."

McGill's vision also directed his energy and allowed many of his changes to be implemented. He commented: "I have a very clear vision—it's almost absolute. I take situations that are happening today and see whether they fit into my vision. The downside is that I have a total intolerance for things that don't fit into the vision. I'll reject them out of hand. . . . The more you can get people to focus, the more successful you'll be."

Notice how the word *intolerance* pops up. One can only wonder if a man bent on implementing a strong and unconventional vision cannot help but antagonize powerful others who might hold different views. "Through our research, we nailed down the facts. Then we confronted based on the facts. In corporate policy meetings, we move our themes into the presentations. These were very strong sessions, sometimes brutally challenging people," said McGill as he described his sessions with senior management. In his desire to bring change, the charismatic often alienates the forces that represent the status quo. These vested interests may unify and later mobilize against the leader.

If we think back to AT&T, we see that it is largely a culture built on consensus and cooperation, not one of contention. McGill's challenges were countercultural and unconventional. He not only introduced a new way of looking at the future that was more market-oriented but also new ways of behaving and approaching problems. This unconventionality is a hallmark of the charismatic leader. Its advantage is that the traditions, norms, and values that have stood in the way of necessary change are challenged and overthrown. But the guardians of these traditions will feel threatened. As well, some charismatics may seek change and unconventionality for its own sake rather than for beneficial purposes. Actions made in the name of change by the charismatic can sometimes be like a tidal wave that takes everything in its path—changing both the bad and the good.

Like many charismatics, McGill was also a preacher. He preached the gospel of his vision. Preachers tend to attract disciples. Subordinates, in reality, become followers. And followers in an organization are a matter of concern. The issue is power—for not only is the charismatic making things happen but he is attracting a devoted following and drawing more and more attention to himself. As the leader gains greater influence and begins to challenge senior management and peers, problems arise. Thus a charismatic leader, especially one within an organization not of his own creation, acts both to magnetize his subordinates and sometimes to repulse his peers and superiors. Like a foreign organism in the human body, eventually the charismatic is surrounded by antibodies that may attempt to finish him off. The *Wall Street Journal,* in commenting on McGill's departure from AT&T, said: "American Bell's first months have been marked by organizational problems and less-than-expected sales results. Some company observers said that while Mr. McGill couldn't be held accountable for many of those problems, he had upset AT&T's top management with overly optimistic business forecasts and a series of clashes with other executives" (White, 1983, p. 4).

There are other dilemmas with charismatics. Many of them, for example, love the "big picture." They are foremost conceptualizers and promoters. Dee Hock, the first CEO of Visa (the credit card's parent organization), "conceptualized" his organization's mission as "the world's premier electronic payment system where any consumer can place his surplus value (savings) in any institution of his choice in any form he chooses and be able to exchange those resources for any services or good he chooses anywhere in the world 24 hours a day" (James, 1981, p. 16). This is a far more global role for Visa than the task of administering credit card services. But the advantage of such a broad conceptualization is that it dramatically expands the company's purpose. It also heightens employees' sensitivity to opportunities beyond today's credit card services. The disadvantage is that the leader can be foremost a conceptualizer rather than an administrator. To succeed, conceptualizers must surround themselves with others who are good on execution and detail. Some have an aversion to formal organizing. They freely skip levels and poke their heads in on their subordinates' work. More important, many, though not all, seem to create love/hate feelings with their subordinates. They are tough and demanding, yet the reward of their praise is so confirming that subordinates describe it as an "emotional high" and, therefore, work hard for their leader's commendation. As a result, motivation and task accomplishment often exceed all expectations. But praise and rewards may soon become an addiction that, when denied, can make subordinates feel like outcasts. A co-worker of McGill's stated: "He is a very loyal boss if he likes you. But if he doesn't, you're dead in three minutes" ("AT&T Unit's McGill Resigns . . . ," June 8, 1983, p. 26).

These are but a few of the issues surrounding the charismatic leader that I will explore throughout this book. As the reader can see from this initial case, charismatic leaders are a potent force and one that, if not managed properly, can create serious problems for themselves and their organizations. And while there is a "sweet and sour" quality about many charismatic leaders, there is little question that their abilities at creating and revitalizing organizations are unique among leaders. In times of great uncertainty and difficulty, they may be just the leader an organization or a society is looking for. Indeed, a serious lack of these leaders may be causing some of the big problems facing North American industry today, especially the slow pace of change in many of our larger organizations. For a moment, then, let us consider the positive side of charismatic leadership and why we may need such leaders despite their potential liabilities.

The Need for Quantum Changes

Although these are times of great uncertainty and upheaval, they are also times ripe for special kinds of leaders. By "special" I am referring to leaders who are masters of change, who can inspire us to take risks, and who possess a keen sense of strategic opportunity. Charismatic leaders possess such qualities. Certainly there are many other types of leaders who might fit the bill, but organizations may need radical change—and the ordinary leader is generally incapable of inducing it.

Recent research shows that organizations can get so immersed in their own inertia that they often require revolutionary changes to adapt successfully. (See Starbuck, Greve, and Hedberg, 1978; Miller and Friesen, 1980, 1984; Hannan and Freeman, 1984; Tushman and Romanelli, 1985.) In other words, many organizations may not actually be able to change in spite of warnings from their environment. Instead, once an organization implements its strategies and various structures, it tends to be maintained by its own momentum. As opportunities and challenges shift within the marketplace, this momentum creates an inertia. This, in turn, causes organizations to persist with their present approach despite the risk of becoming ultimately ineffective. Organizations, then, essentially fail to learn more effective ways of dealing with their environment. As a result, "quantum" changes are eventually required to correct the damage brought about by lengthy periods of inertia. Hence successful change does not come in a gradual, incremental way but in a tumultuous and radical manner.

Sadly these quantum changes seem to occur only after a significant decline in performance (Tushman, Virany, and Romanelli, 1987). Poor performance forces the organization to adapt or die. And to adapt, a new leader must often be brought in to initiate the direction of change. Interestingly, the truly major changes seem to occur if the leader is recruited from outside the organization. (See Helmich and Brown, 1972; Helmich, 1975, 1978; Reinganum, 1985; House and Singh, 1987.) This is largely because leaders from the outside appear to bring a new way of seeing the world. They are not trapped in the very norms and conventions that have created the inertia in the first place. Since these figures are more willing to buck the system, they are more likely to induce quantum changes.

Chrysler is a good illustration. By the late 1970s, poor management and inertia had led to a serious decline in the company's performance. By 1978, its most senior managers appeared to recognize that they themselves could not resolve the growing problems. Chrysler was entering a crisis. On the day Lee Iacocca assumed the presidency, Chrysler would report its greatest loss for any quarter in its history. Upon his arrival, Iacocca would discover a top-heavy bureaucracy comprised of thirty-five vice-presidents. Each worked independently with virtually no communication between manufacturing, sales, and marketing. The company had no integrated system of financial controls or proper financial planning. It was impossible to obtain accurate information on the profitability of individual operations—information that Iacocca had found critical to effective management at Ford. With sales in decline, the company was also seriously overstaffed. Its product line was largely outdated, and the few popular models were in short supply.

Iacocca's approach to resolving this crisis was not a gradual, incremental process. He began by replacing senior managers. After a trial period, he found that Chrysler's vice-presidents were unable to adapt to the changes he envisioned. The comments of a colleague of Iacocca's illustrate the concern: "These people have learned the Chrysler way of running their own show. They will never adjust. It's too late" (Iacocca and Novak, 1984, p. 156). Iacocca would replace all but two of the thirty-five vice-presidents.

He soon had in place a quarterly review process and had revamped the financial organization. He downsized the organization and laid off thousands of workers. Selling peripheral businesses and closing plants, he raised badly needed cash. He introduced a union representative onto the board and a profit-sharing stock option plan for employees. A new line of cars, the K cars, was put into production. Later a new minivan would appear.

In an extremely short period of time, Iacocca instituted perhaps more radical change at Chrysler than the company had seen since its founding. By 1983, these changes had transformed the company's record losses into a $925 million profit—the largest in the company's history. But it had taken an outsider who was a charismatic leader—and one well versed in the industry and willing to introduce quantum changes—to transform Chrysler.

The Bureaucratic Mentality

Very few leaders can induce the major changes that organizations require. Due to the training and experience these executives receive, they simply are unable to develop or even appreciate the revolutionary vision needed to transform their organization. They are caught in a web of structures, politics, and traditions that do not permit them a more radical vantage point.

Because organizations, especially large ones, consist of bureaucracies with pools of highly specialized managers and executives, these individuals have very precise roles where duties and regulations are narrowly prescribed. A constricted understanding of one's task is emphasized instead of a broad vision of how things could be. As a manager moves up the hierarchy, he or she is rewarded for being effective within this narrow range of responsibility and authority. As a result, there is no encouragement to develop a wide perspective on the organization's purpose or its market. Managers arrive at the top with a myopic sense of the world that is difficult to reverse. Yet to be sensitive to strategic opportunities and market needs, one needs a broad perspective and a sense of vision.

In one company, a talented research scientist found himself promoted through a series of management positions. At first his responsibilities involved managing other scientists. But eventually he was promoted to head an operating division with added responsibilities for manufacturing, sales, marketing, and finance. The division produced consumer electronics in a highly competitive, rapidly changing market—an area where the executive had no experience. He had little idea of the market opportunities for his division, and he had little idea of the critical need to integrate the division's different functions given the quick pace of change. He had grown up managing R&D labs. By the end of his first year, the division's sales had slipped 20 percent, profits by 35 percent. Within two years, the division was operating at a loss and the parent organization was contemplating the sale of the unit. Interviews with division managers traced the problem to their leader's lack of strategic vision and his underestimation of the role of marketing in consumer electronics. In this case, a specialized manager had been promoted to a general manager's position with inadequate training and experience.

Bureaucracies emphasize control. Since initiative by the lower ranks is often seen as a challenge to authority, it is purposely minimized by the confines of a narrowly defined job. Leadership is discouraged. When one is finally called upon to lead, he or she has had little experience and is accustomed to taking orders, not giving them.

Moreover, bureaucracies discourage risk taking. To a certain extent their conservatism is in response to the need for short-term performance such as strong quarterly earnings, a constraint that discourages investment in anything but the sure bet. Innovation, on the other hand, entails risk and costs. Yet for the long-term health of an organization, innovation and risk taking must pervade all levels of the organization, especially in highly competitive environments.

Finally, bureaucracies reward people for being team players, for accepting the norms and rules of the organization and for playing by the politics of the firm. Radical perspectives that challenge the status quo are seen as too unconventional and are disregarded. To some extent this is a reasonable response: *Too many* innovative and unconventional actions can indeed be disruptive. But while unconventionality and innovation can be costly and risky, the price that is paid is more often an inability to see or accept change. There is more than a little truth in Machiavelli's comment: "Change has no constituency."

All these forces conspire to transform potential leadership into mere managership. The caretaker is more important than the risk-taker. By the time they reach executivehood, young managers have been trained to see the world, their markets, and their organizations too narrowly. They have also been taught to eschew risk. Their corporate strategies, therefore, maintain the status quo or reflect caution rather than vision. And so the cycle of bureaucracy perpetuates itself.

Consider the remarks of the CEO of one large chemical company to management researcher Robert Lamb (1987). Lamb asked the executive (p. 11) whether he had had a strategic plan when he became chief executive:

> No, I did not. I think as with most corporate executives, of our corporation at least, I was a career employee. I graduated from college and knocked on the door of the employment lobby—even at that point in time I didn't have a clear idea of my assets or what I could do in a company. I was totally dependent on them for a career path. Fortu-

nately, they put me in an area where I had an interest and could use the skills I had. I grew up in the organization. . . . I'd probably have to say that I was molded in terms of my attitudes toward certain things and what the principles of the company should be and what was, perhaps, important. These were just imbued in me in the beginning, and so by the time I reached the chairman's job the philosophy I had probably agreed with my predecessors'.

The executive was then asked why his firm had recently diversified into cosmetics: "The cosmetics thing was fortuitous. The company said that maybe if we do something else, cosmetics might be a logical extension of our activities. . . . It did utilize the same production base and you could stretch your imagination to a time when research and development might make a contribution. We didn't have the guts to really initiate anything. . . . [Our bank] came to us and said, 'Why don't you buy?' And so we were forced to make a decision" (p. 11).

In a mature organization like this, the firm's culture and bureaucracy now define what "leadership" and its strategic objectives will be and, in turn, they perpetuate the values, assumptions, and ways of operating in the world that have traditionally characterized the organization. If the organization is to change, a leader must break the tyranny of both. Leaders from inside the organization can be effective only if they are objective and understand these forces. But often senior managers are unwilling or unable to provide the radical break that is necessary. For these very reasons, leadership with an outsider's perspective is needed to induce transformation. New or unconventional leaders can bring about just such shifts, especially if they are at the top of the organization. But not just any outsider will do. There is evidence that outsiders who are unfamiliar with the organization's industry, its products, its technologies, and, for that matter, its culture, many times fail (Kotter, 1982; Schein, 1985). Rather outsiders must be adept change masters who can assess and redefine an organization's culture and skilled strategists who can mesh the company's resources and talent with markets.

The Right Business Culture

But it is not just an organization's bureaucracy that inhibits inspirational leaders from developing—it is our general business culture. Let me provide an example. To transform, leaders must have a depth of experience within their industries, an extensive network of cooperative relationships throughout their companies and industries, the ability to organize both people and resources, skills of strategic vision, a talent at persuasion, and the ability to motivate and inspire. That is quite a list of skills and abilities for a single individual. Even so, many superior managers do possess the first several qualities. The remaining traits, however, are far rarer. Why? Our society's business culture and our educational system have not encouraged the development of skills of vision, persuasion, or inspiration. A manager's potential to be visionary is lost through years of tactical focus. In business schools, analytic skills, not creativity, are trained. In corporations, persuasion and inspiration are rarely rewarded as managerial skills. Our emphasis on rule by hierarchy and the chain of command have eliminated the need for persuading others or inspiring others to work. Yet to induce quantum changes, leaders must be able to view their markets and organizations in new and visionary ways and be able to pry employees loose from their attachment to the status quo. They must inspire them to take risks in revolutionizing their organizations. They must become adept managers of organizational culture.

Skills of persuasion and inspiration are especially important in motivating organizations to change. Leaders who strike a motivating chord in the "hearts and souls" of their employees appear more often able to induce change—whereas the majority of business leaders present themselves and their organizational goals in almost "anti-emotional" ways. As Robert B. Horton, CEO of British Petroleum America and chairman of Standard Oil, commented: "You cannot be an effective business leader on calm analysis alone. Nobody will follow a turnip. To lead you need passion . . . ardor, zeal, enthusiasm—this personal involvement is absolutely necessary in a good leader. We need this

quality called by Lyndon Johnson, I believe, 'fire in the belly' "
(Horton, 1988, p. 13). Skills of vision, persuasion, inspiration,
are critical, therefore, yet missing in most businesses today.

These qualities become particularly critical in getting organizational members dissatisfied with the status quo and actually yearning for change. Indeed, dissatisfaction is an essential
ingredient in transforming an organization. A leader must be
able to convince subordinates that there is good reason to seek
change. The present, despite its problems, is a seductively secure
environment for many employees. Change is often far more
threatening. Leaders must develop in subordinates a sense of
discomfort and unrest with the present. At the same time, they
must instill a sense of confidence and longing for an image of
the future that will lead employees to turn their backs on the
certainty of the status quo.

Leadership Skills Today

Do our business leaders of today have these skills? The
answer appears to be no. Again, part of the problem is how
managers are socialized. As noted, they are taught to think narrowly. Their organizational cultures reinforce often outdated
assumptions about the firm and its markets. As also noted, business leaders, especially in large organizations, are not expected
to be passionate about their ideas or inspirational. Executives
are not expected to be visionaries or orators. Some are even put
off by the very idea. But the workplace and the marketplace
have changed. Employees today are seeking more meaning in
their work. They are better educated. Their expectations are
higher. They have greater influence. The world, moreover, is far
more competitive so that change and innovation must become
an everyday affair.

Apart from socialization and cultural problems, the functional background of today's CEOs is a problem. Since the
1960s, CEOs have been chosen principally from the ranks of
managers with financial experience. As a result, a company's financial strategy has become its main focus. A recent study of
executives (Lamb, 1987) found that most CEOs stressed this as

their main function. Financial strategizing has become the substitute for a comprehensive corporate strategy. As a result of this obsession with finances, the company becomes a portfolio of assets. Mergers and acquisitions become the means for growth and investment, and quarterly earnings and stock prices become the focus of attention. Many of these executives described the inordinate amount of time they spent daily on finances even though such tasks are delegated to a financial officer. As one CEO stated: "I'm being held accountable financially. I'm being measured against a series of financial yardsticks by institutional investors, lenders, and, in some cases, by creditors and suppliers and major customers and insurers as never before. With all these financial tests they run on this company and we run on ourselves, it's a wonder we squeeze out enough time to actually make, sell, and deliver our product" (Lamb, 1987, pp. 108–109).

To a certain extent this emphasis on finance has made sense. The 1980s were the "decade of restructuring" with its takeover threats, global competition, rapid technological change, and deregulation; financial health and leanness were critical to survival. But while the emphasis on finance has helped some firms to become more effective, its long-term effects can be crippling. In firms driven by financial strategies, marketing is often allowed to decline, risky technological projects are cut, and the creation of a more dedicated management team is abandoned for the analysis of finances and the manipulation of investments (Lamb, 1987, p. 133). Quality can suffer. The *Economist* recently commented: "A Western quest for instant financial return that once bred wealth . . . has drifted towards shortcuts and shabbiness."

These background trends and the other forces I have cited have led to a general weakening of the leader's role as the source of strategic innovation and change. As a result, the antiquated worldviews of an organization can persist unchallenged. Yet *Fortune*, in describing the decade of restructuring, comments that for the 1990s "the principal challenge will be innovation. . . . If there is one skill that every business unit should have these days, the experts say, it is the ability to innovate, to devise new products and services and ways to make and deliver them" (Kiechel, 1988, p. 42). But for this to happen there must be individuals who are willing to buck convention, who have a broad strategic vision, and who are skillful persuaders and motivators. Enter the charismatic leader.

Enter the Charismatic Leader

If leadership can play a vital role in creating change, certain leaders are better at it than others. Historically we find that charismatic leaders have always personified the forces of change, unconventionality, vision, and an entrepreneurial spirit. (See Bass, 1985; Conger, 1985; Weber, 1947; Willner, 1984.) Leaders from the traditional mold are temperamentally disposed toward lower levels of risk, preferring to administer rather than to truly lead, and more inclined toward the pragmatic rather than the visionary. These qualities rarely provide a hothouse for innovation. Creativity demands intuition, uncertainty, unconventionality, and individual expression. Management, in the traditional sense, runs counter to these qualities with its emphasis on the rational, the status quo, certainty, and consensus.

Lee Iacocca, for instance, was not willing to accept the traditions of Chrysler or, for that matter, those of his industry. Instead he chose to break with convention. He dropped his first year salary to one dollar, obtained massive government-backed loans, introduced money-back guarantees on cars, brought union representation onto the board, and appeared in advertisements featuring Chrysler products. All were highly unconventional actions for the automobile industry, yet ultimately they were effective tactics for revitalizing Chrysler.

The charismatic leader embodies many more of these creative forces. Like Arch McGill, these leaders are tireless challengers of the status quo—relentless in their search for new approaches to problems and markets. As well, they are skillful masters of motivation—able to foster a deep sense of commitment and drive among subordinates who then attempt to achieve the seemingly inachievable. John Sculley, CEO of Apple Computer, described these qualities as those of an "impresario." Reflecting on his first meeting with Steven Jobs, the founder of

Apple Computer, he commented that leadership for the charismatic Jobs was a creative and inspirational process:

> When I walked through the Macintosh [computer]
> building with Steve, it became clear that he wasn't
> just another general manager bringing a visitor along
> to meet another group of employees. He and many
> of Apple's leaders weren't managers at all; they
> were impresarios. . . . Not unlike the director of an
> opera company, the impresario must cleverly deal
> with the creative temperaments of artists. At times
> he may coach because he knows that creativity is a
> learning process, not a management process. Other
> times he may scold because he knows that creativ-
> ity requires a demanding commitment of self. The
> impresario must be alternately tough and admiring
> toward his people. In art, he ensures that the set-
> ting and stage are conducive to the production of a
> masterpiece. His gift is to merge powerful ideas
> with the performance of his artists. At Apple, we
> bring together a company of artists; we build the
> infrastructure of set designers, stagehands, and a
> supporting cast; and we applaud the performances
> of our cast members, who oftentimes emerge as
> stars on their own. This is the difference between
> inspiring the growing numbers of "knowledge work-
> ers" in our economy and simply motivating people.
> . . . Getting people to reach beyond their best abil-
> ities is knowing how to manage creativity. [Scully,
> 1987b, pp. 114-115]

Because of their creativity, inspiration, unconventionality,
and vision, charismatic leaders are potential sources of enormous transformation for organizations. If managed well, charismatics can be of great help to organizations seeking to adapt to
changing environments, for they challenge the forces that blunt
expressions of strategic vision and an inspired work force.

While I have spoken largely about the role of charismatic

leaders in transforming mature organizations, I would be remiss in not drawing the reader's attention to the equally vital role these leaders play in the creation of organizations. Many of the famous entrepreneurs of this decade have been charismatic leaders—for example, Mary Kay Ash of Mary Kay Cosmetics, Ross Perot of Electronic Data Systems, Donald Burr of People Express, and Fred Smith of Federal Express. It is again their positive orientation toward risk, an unusual ability to see opportunity, a drive to innovate, and a masterful ability at persuading and motivating that leads these figures to be successful entrepreneurs.

As well, their skill at selling their ideas is instrumental in the initial success of their ventures. They are very adept at persuasion—especially at persuading investors. John DeLorean was able to raise hundreds of millions of dollars for his automobile venture thanks to his powers of persuasion. *Inc.* magazine noted that Steven Jobs's greatest impact in the start-up of Apple was in his wheeling and dealing: "Where Jobs's oratory really made a difference was in his determination to put Apple on equal footing with the established giants. He was able to cut competitive purchasing deals, for instance, that were simply unheard of for a 'who they?' start-up. . . . Apple thus became the little computer company that thought like a big computer company" (Kahn, 1984, p. 83).

The entrepreneurial sectors of the country are vitally important. Small businesses, not large corporations, are responsible for the bulk of new jobs and for most of the nation's recent economic growth—especially when one considers that they are more productive and innovative (Naisbitt, 1984). In 1987 alone, the three largest corporations in North America laid off one million workers—whereas since 1981, 100 percent of the net new American jobs have come from small businesses (*Economist*, p. 15, Feb. 6, 1988). For this very reason, we should be more committed to developing skills associated with charismatic leadership and entrepreneurship in our business education programs today.

In their roles as entrepreneurs or catalysts of change for large organizations, charismatic leaders have much to teach us.

They have a unique ability to see strategic opportunities, take risks, foster change, persuade and motivate. All of these are vital skills for leaders today. In the following chapters, I will show how they do what they do so skillfully. I will also try to be realistic. For charismatic leaders bring with them a set of liabilities that we will also explore. Charismatics are not always the appropriate leaders for organizations; sometimes they can be more disruptive than constructive.

Our interest in charismatic leadership should not focus so much on how our managers can become charismatic leaders as on what we can learn from the strengths of these special leaders to promote more effective leadership in general. We may not *want* more charismatic leaders. Apart from the risks associated with these figures, there is another issue: Not all of us have the disposition to become charismatic leaders. Moreover, I fear that certain personalities will become ensnared by the connotations of power and attention that go with the image of a charismatic leader. There is a great deal of glamour associated with being charismatic. Yet we certainly do not need more narcissistic leaders. What we need instead are managers who are better leaders—men and women who can draw on the skills of charismatic leaders to see strategic opportunities, to encourage change and innovation, to persuade and motivate. It is not the leader's "charisma," per se, that is so important but his or her abilities. In the following chapters we will discover just what these skills are.

Chapter 2

What Makes the Charismatic Difference

While we may not have the definitive answer to the secret of charisma, we have learned in recent years a great deal about the qualities that lead people to describe someone as a charismatic leader. This chapter explains what we know and explores the process by which we attribute charisma to certain people. Before we begin, however, I want to spend a moment examining why the word *charisma* has been so elusive. This will help us grasp why charismatic leaders themselves have been so poorly understood.

The Mystery of Charisma

Why is charisma so mysterious? Charismatic individuals are certainly not subatomic particles invisible to the human eye. Quite to the contrary, they are exceptionally visible. We read books about them and see them featured in the press and television news. Why is it, then, that you and I are not able to pinpoint the qualities that make up a person's charisma?

Several years ago, I set out to tackle this question. After a great deal of probing, I have come to the conclusion that two

21

elements contribute to the charismatic mystique. The first involves charisma's links to human perception. If you compare various charismatic leaders, you will find that they often have quite different personalities—Adolf Hitler and Franklin D. Roosevelt, for example. One can hardly imagine two more different people. Now if there were in fact a single charismatic personality, then Americans too would have perceived Adolf Hitler as charismatic and Germans would have regarded Roosevelt in a similar light. What we find instead is that one person's charismatic leader is not necessarily another's. So the answer is not a single personality type but something more complex. Other forces are at play, and not all of them involve the leader per se. Instead they are intimately tied to a process we call attribution. Essentially, you and I interpret behavior from our own subjective experience. When we witness a person's behavior, some of us will interpret it as charismatic and others not. This is largely because of our different needs and backgrounds. The exact mechanics of this process will be explained shortly. At this point, just note that we each experience the world differently and, as a result, we may interpret the actions of others differently.

The second component of charisma's mystique is the history of the word itself. The term is actually an ancient Greek word meaning "gift," in particular a gift from the gods. Powers that could not be explained by ordinary means were called *charismata.* The term was later picked up by the Christian church to describe talents such as prophecy, wisdom, and healing believed to have been bestowed by God. The term would probably have remained forever restricted to the church were it not for an early-twentieth-century German sociologist, Max Weber. In scanning history, he had found that from time to time a single individual could revolutionize political authority not by the power of tradition or law but by the sheer force of his or her personality. Weber argued that the authority of these figures stemmed from their "charisma," a gift that set them apart from ordinary men and caused them to be "treated as endowed with supernatural, superhuman, or at least . . . exceptional powers and qualities . . . not accessible to the ordinary person, but . . .

of divine origin or as exemplary" (1947, pp. 358–359). Weber retained much of the original Christian meaning of charisma and as a by-product perpetuated the mystique surrounding the source of a leader's charisma. He used charismatic authority only as an *ideal*—in other words, as a simplified and accentuated model of reality.

Despite his sketchy outline of charismatic leadership, Weber's ideas intrigued social scientists. A decade after translations of his work (1947) appeared in North America, political scientists and sociologists became so fascinated by his ideas that they spent the 1960s and 1970s exploring and debating the sources of a leader's "charisma." They undertook historical studies of the great political leaders of the twentieth century such as Castro, Hitler, and Kennedy in hopes of finding a universal "charismatic personality." But this hope quickly faded as the search for qualities common to all these leaders yielded inconclusive results (Dow, 1969; Willner, 1984). Instead, researchers found variations so great that a single charismatic personality seemed highly improbable. Nonetheless, the term became popular, and people began using the label freely to describe any leader who could arouse emotions and inspire. Research, however, proceeded slowly on the topic. It would not be until sometime later that studies of both political and organizational leaders would reveal what we know today (Willner, 1984; Conger and Kanungo, 1988d).

How We Attribute Charisma to Others

When the concept of a charismatic personality proved a dead end, attention turned to *behavior* that might create the perception of charisma rather than specific personality characteristics. This avenue proved more fruitful. Researchers found that certain types of behavior could indeed lead people to perceive a leader as charismatic (see Willner, 1984). It was discovered, however, that in order for these behaviors to induce the perception of charisma, their specific character has to be seen by followers as *relevant* to their situation. If followers do not think their leader's formulation of a strategic vision matches their own aspirations, they are less likely to perceive him or her as a charismatic leader.

The dynamics of this process are explained by attribution theory. Basically, attribution theory holds that you and I search for the meaning of people's behavior. (See, for example, Heider, 1944, 1958; Kelley, 1972, 1973.) We are what might be called *naive psychologists*—ordinary people trying to understand other people's behavior. We wish to determine what certain kinds of behavior tell us about a person's underlying character and, as a group or a society, we have learned, formally or informally, to associate certain behavior with certain labels of character. Suppose we see a woman acting very aggressively in the checkout line at the supermarket. As a society we have developed assumptions about what constitutes aggressive behavior, and when we see that behavior in action we label the person as aggressive. These labels then help us predict and understand human behavior.

But how does this concept apply to leadership? In a similar way, each of us holds a set of theories of what behavior is associated with different kinds of leaders. These theories are based on our own experience and the society, culture, or organization in which we live and work. In North America, for example, leaders who are dictatorial, power-hungry, and shrewd might be called "tyrannical" because we share a theory of the behavior that characterizes a tyrannical leader. Hence we believe that a certain type of leadership, whether tyrannical or charismatic, produces a specific set of behavior (see Calder, 1977, p. 198).

Attribution theory has two important implications for our understanding of charismatic leaders. First, we must discover which behavior leads to shared perceptions of charisma in our society. This is the task that social scientists have been carrying out for the last several decades and is an essential function of this book. Second, we must recognize that we interpret behavior according to our own personal experience or situation. What one person might perceive as strategic vision, for example, another might not. What appears as the unconventional behavior of wearing jeans and a T-shirt to the office in one organization might be completely conventional behavior in another.

Behavior is attributed relative to the beholder's context. Although unconventional behavior and long-range vision are characteristics of a charismatic leader, their specific quality or content will determine whether they are perceived as such. Adolf Hitler's strategic vision of a German fatherland spreading throughout Europe heightened his charismatic appeal for many Germans in the 1930s, yet it did not hold the same appeal for Americans, Britons, or German Jews. His message, his goals, his behavior, did not fit *their* aspirations. Their notion of an inspiring strategic vision was certainly not the message articulated by Hitler.

Each dimension of charismatic behavior—whether strategic vision, unconventionality, or something else—has to be meaningful in the context at hand. If not, it is unlikely to be perceived as a charismatic quality. Understanding charismatic leadership involves pinpointing the leader's specific behavior and then assessing how it affects the perceptions of followers—in our case, in a North American context.

The Behavioral Dimension of Charisma

Now we can turn to the most important question: What behavior distinguishes charismatic leaders from others? I will begin with a simple model that defines leadership as the process of moving an organization from an existing state to some future state through four stages. This model applies principally to the top management of an organization. (Our discussion throughout this book will focus principally on leadership at these levels.)

In Stage One, the leader must assess the current situation in terms of strategic opportunities, constraints, resources, and the needs of the organization. This is an ongoing process. Since environments are in a constant state of flux, the leader never stops scanning the marketplace and making and remaking strategic and organizational decisions. After each evaluation, the leader formulates or reformulates a set of strategies and goals that seem right for the situation at hand. These two processes are inextricably intertwined—one naturally leading to the other. This is Stage One: the formulation of goals.

In Stage Two the leader sets about communicating and interpreting these goals in ways that are meaningful, given the organization's aims. He or she may use a variety of means including public speeches, one-on-one discussions, company strategic documents, the annual report, memos, and so on. He or she may communicate the goals by persuasion or by direct order. Ultimately, however, the manner in which he describes his goals will affect the motivation of his organization to implement them.

In Stages Three and Four the leader builds commitment and trust in him- or herself and his or her goals and demonstrates how these goals can be achieved by the organization. He or she may exemplify the behavior and attitudes that are necessary for success, devise specific tactics, and create a system of values and decision rules that organizational members can follow. Like any model, these stages are a drastic simplification of what is, in fact, a complex and interactive process among the leader, the management team, the organization, and the environment. Leadership is rarely such a neat chronological progression of activities. Instead, activities "down the line" may influence those that come before. Nonetheless, this framework captures enough of the dynamics of leading to help us effectively examine the differences between charismatic and noncharismatic leadership at the senior levels of an organization. Let us now take a closer look at how we distinguish charismatic leaders along these four dimensions (see Figure 1).

Stage One: Sensing Opportunity and Formulating a Vision. Research suggests that charismatic leaders possess two skills characterizing this stage which, when combined, often set them apart from other leaders. (See Bass, 1985; Conger and Kanungo, 1988a; House, Woycke, and Fodor, 1988.) The first is a sensitivity to their constituents' needs. Constituents, in this case, may comprise both members of the leader's organization and his customers. The second quality is an unusual ability to see the deficiencies of the existing situation as well as the untapped opportunities. Mahatma Gandhi acutely sensed the Indian people's need to sever their ties to England; he sensed that British rule was failing to achieve a longed-for sense of freedom.

Figure 1. Stages in Charismatic Leadership.

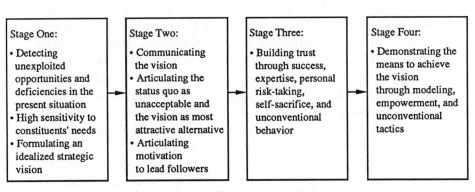

Stage One:	Stage Two:	Stage Three:	Stage Four:
• Detecting unexploited opportunities and deficiencies in the present situation • High sensitivity to constituents' needs • Formulating an idealized strategic vision	• Communicating the vision • Articulating the status quo as unacceptable and the vision as most attractive alternative • Articulating motivation to lead followers	• Building trust through success, expertise, personal risk-taking, self-sacrifice, and unconventional behavior	• Demonstrating the means to achieve the vision through modeling, empowerment, and unconventional tactics

Source: Adapted from Conger and Kanungo (1988a).

Dr. Edwin Land, inventor of the Polaroid camera, recognized the technological and market opportunity for a product that did not exist at the time—instant photography. Steven Jobs of Apple Computer detected the need for a low-priced, "user-friendly" personal computer—again a product existing largely as an idea at the time. In all three cases, the charismatic leader discerned a need among his constituents.

So a charismatic entrepreneur may more readily discern unexploited needs in the marketplace and transform them into new products and services as in the case of Edwin Land. Significant shortcomings in an organization are likely to serve as platforms for radical change as with Lee Iacocca at Chrysler. In sum, then, charismatic leaders are highly sensitive to any situation that presents a need for major change or offers unexploited opportunities. (Because this is often a trait of entrepreneurs in general, the qualities described in the next three stages are likely to be the key characteristics distinguishing charismatic and non-charismatic entrepreneurs.)

Given their sensitivity to deficiencies, charismatic leaders in mature organizations are therefore most likely to be agents of radical change. Note, however, that the outcome of the changes they advocate is not what generally leads to their charisma. Rather it is simply the actions taken to bring about change that are important. As George Gallup commented, "People tend to judge a man by his goals, by what he's trying to do, and not necessarily by what he accomplishes or by how well he succeeds" (Edelman, 1964, p. 78). Given this orientation to change, charismatic leaders can always be distinguished from managers, administrators, and other leaders who tend to maintain the status quo or advocate incremental rather than revolutionary change. For this reason, charismatic leaders tend to play a vital role in inducing quantum changes in organizations.

Bob Lipp, a former president of Chemical Bank and one of my research participants, illustrates this sensitivity to constituents and the use of radical change to address problems. In 1977, Lipp was promoted to direct the retail banking operations of Chembank. Within five years he had astonishingly doubled retail and small business deposits from $1 billion to $2 billion. In addition, he had turned losses in 1977 into an after-tax profit of $85 million in 1981—accounting for 40 to 50 percent of Chemical Bank's overall earnings for that year.

To understand these dramatic changes, a little history is necessary. Prior to 1972, each of the branch operations had responsibility not only for retail accounts but also for large corporate clients within their districts. In time, branch managers began to devote more and more attention to big clients while neglecting the personal and small business accounts. In 1972, the corporation decided to correct this bias by centralizing commercial accounts over $5 million into commercial district centers, leaving the branches with only retail operations. The branches, as one executive described it, became only "a necessary evil to gather deposits." The branch managers were greatly demoralized by their loss in status and responsibility, and the effectiveness of the operations would soon deteriorate. This is the moment Lipp stepped in.

Lipp quickly sensed the dilemma. He believed he could restore a sense of significance as well as profitability to the operations. His objective was to create recognition within the bank that the retail operations were important. As Lipp explained: "I saw that the branch system was very down; morale was low. There were serious problems and a lot of staff were just hiding. What I saw was that we really wanted to create a small community for each branch where customers would feel known. To do that, I knew I needed to create an attitude change. . . . I knew I had to change their [branch managers] mentality from being lost in a bureaucracy to feeling like the president of their own bank. I also knew that the way to get business was to go out and ask for it." He radically transformed the branch manager's position into one with greater authority and discretion. Managers were now responsible for branch deposits and controlled their day-to-day activities. Simultaneously, Lipp revamped goals, responsibilities, compensation, and measurement systems to implement his plan and bolster morale. Ultimately these changes proved highly effective. The critical point is that Lipp detected his subordinates' needs very accurately and then devised certain radical changes to address them. An administrator in this leadership role would perhaps have attempted incremental changes such as restoring profitability by cutting manpower or closing down certain branches. In either case, he would have failed to recognize the essential problem and probably would not have addressed subordinates' needs as a central focus.

Stage Two: Articulating the Vision. In the second stage, charismatic leaders tend to be different from others because of their goals and the way in which they communicate them. Usually they are characterized by a profound sense of strategic vision. (Here we refer to vision as an idealized future goal that the leader wishes the organization to achieve.) Generally their goals tend to be idealized and challenge the status quo (see Bass, 1985, Conger and Kanungo, 1988a, and House and others, 1988). As a result, subordinates are likely to perceive the leader's goals as extraordinary vision rather than ordinary goals. By presenting utopian goals to followers, the leader provides a sense of tremendous challenge and motivation for change. Since the vision is a perspective shared by the followers and promises to meet their aspirations, it tends to be very acceptable despite its radical departure from the present situation.

In articulating their goals, charismatic leaders are also likely to differ from others along two important dimensions. The first is the way in which they *describe* their vision. Charismatics begin by describing the current situation as unacceptable. In this sense they strive to create dissatisfaction. This is a critical step in every successful change process. One charismatic leader I studied, president of an operating division of a *Fortune* 500 company, commented on this tactic: "Nothing can happen until the need for change translates into an actual awareness of that need. You often have to force that awareness. First of all, you have to make people uncomfortable. There are a lot of funny things running around in people's heads distracting them from 'what is' reality. You have to get people to see the 'what is,' to see reality, to see that they're not contributing to the best of their abilities, and to see that the product's inferior. You must lay out whatever the reality is. Then you have to get them to buy into your vision."

Jan Carlzon, the charismatic president of the Scandinavian Airlines System (SAS), often used this practice to mobilize his organization. Carlzon is noted for his dramatic turnaround of SAS, which was losing $17 million a year when he assumed the presidency in 1981. By the end of 1987, it had achieved pretax profits of $256 million. In describing his vision for SAS, he would employ a tactic of publicly arguing that a new era of competition would soon be upon Sweden's airlines. In reality, this "new era" was not so apparent or, for that matter, as radical as Carlzon would describe it. But this is how he portrayed the situation:

> Many people were quick to opine that free competition will never hit the European airline industry. "You are crying wolf," they accused me, "and that is tantamount to manipulating your employees." To them I say: If the competition stays at about the same level as it is today, then we can handle it without having to do anything special. But if we improve our efficiency, then we'll be even stronger in the future. If competition is opened a limited amount and we haven't prepared ourselves, we could be in trouble. But if we take steps now, then we won't have to play a risky game of catch-up. If

> competition is completely opened up, we'll cer-
> tainly run into problems if we're caught unawares.
> We'll be faced with crises, panic, cutbacks, layoffs,
> and possibly worse. However, if we are prepared,
> the chances are good that we will fare very well.
> What's more, if SAS is more efficient than any
> other carrier could be, then there will actually be
> no reason for government authorities to open up
> the market. [Carlzon, 1987, p. 132]

Note Carlzon's logic. He argues that a slight amount of increased competition would mean "trouble" and that complete competition would create "crises and panic." He paints a dire picture for his airline if they are not in the least bit prepared and more efficient. But, he argues, if they are well prepared, they can completely preempt any moves toward greater competition. Thus he seems to be saying: "If we work hard, we can have the best of worlds—an efficient airline operating in a noncompetitive environment." He uses the notion of an impending crisis to motivate his organization toward change. This is a scenario described by many of the charismatic leaders I have studied both in mature organizations and in entrepreneurial ventures. Noncharismatic leaders either downplay the negative aspects of the current situation or fail to effectively articulate why the present is intolerable.

At the same time, charismatic leaders describe their future vision as the most attractive and reasonable alternative. And while the vision's goals are often ideals, charismatic leaders describe them as both realistic and attainable. In communicating their vision, they aim to create among subordinates a compelling desire to be led in the direction of the vision despite its often significant hurdles. One way they do this is to link the vision to values that are central for their audience. While the vision's ideals are discrepant because they suggest a radical departure from the present, they simultaneously suggest a return to values that are already cherished. The charismatic leader links these old but important values to future goals in order to heighten their meaningfulness. A subordinate of Arch McGill's described the experience: "Arch has had a vision of the future that, once articulated and put into understandable terms, carried the day for him. The key thing of his leadership is that his vision has allowed him to succeed. If I portray a picture of a compelling and irresistible future for your institution, you are set apart. His vision says to me, as a member of American Bell, that I can make a real difference in society. . . . This is the most exciting ball game in American enterprise today. . . . There is no greater challenge. . . . The key to this country's productivity is in this industry. This company will help sustain the nation as a leader in the world." McGill's vision played to employees' needs to make a significant contribution through their work. More important, it played to deeply held values of national pride in America as a world leader.

The second dimension involves how charismatics communicate their own motivation to lead. In their rhetoric, they may choose words reflecting self-confidence, conviction, expertise, dedication to the cause, and a concern for followers' needs. For example, the charismatic vice-president of a computer company opened a speech to his managers by saying: "Nobody has done what we have done before. We're plowing new ground. We'll do something that nobody else thought was possible. We were 1/1000th the size of IBM, then 1/100th, today we are 1/32nd. There's a strength in this company that pervades. You and I will make the impossible happen." All throughout his talk, his voice exuded confidence and conviction.

These qualities may also be expressed through the leader's behavior, actions, personal appearance, body language, and dress. A leader might appear highly animated to convey a sense of excitement, for instance, or speak in tones that are strong and unwavering. Through these various modes of expression, charismatic leaders communicate their enthusiasm, commitment, and motivation, which in turn become contagious.

Stage Three: Building Trust in the Vision. To be effective as a leader, it is often important that subordinates *desire* the goals the leader proposes. Commitment by coercion or edict is not likely to provide sufficient motivational energy for long-term success. Thus the leader must build exceptional trust among subordinates in himself and in the goals he articulates. The charismatic leader does this through personal risk taking, unconventional expertise, and self-sacrifice. These qualities set the charismatic leader apart from others.

Essentially these leaders attempt to create extraordinary levels of trustworthiness. They accomplish this by showing concern for followers' needs rather than for their own self-interest. This is a critical part of the leadership equation since their goals may involve great uncertainty and risk. To compensate, they must build exceptional trust by demonstrating a total dedication to the cause they share with followers. They may, for instance, engage in acts that demonstrate exemplary levels of commitment and self-sacrifice to achieve the mission's goals. The greater the personal risks taken to achieve the vision, the greater the trustworthiness that is likely to be developed. Lee Iacocca, for example, slashed his salary to a dollar during his first year at Chrysler. Robert Lipp, as head of Chemical Bank's retail operations, traveled to all of his bank's retail branches (approximately two hundred of them) to explain a dramatic turnaround strategy—a remarkable investment of his precious time but an equally remarkable sign of his commitment. John DeLorean, the flamboyant General Motors executive who started his own automobile company, was renowned for his unconventional acts that challenged corporate policy at GM. His actions normally would have caused serious reprimands or have led to lost promotion opportunities. But to subordinates and the public, they were important symbols of his willingness to take risks for what he believed in.

Charismatic leaders may also build trust by appearing as experts. They may demonstrate their knowledge through the visions they formulate and the unconventional tactics they devise. These, in turn, contribute to their aura of extraordinariness. Some degree of demonstrated expertise, such as past successes, may also be necessary. The acceptance of Arch McGill's vision among American Bell's employees, for example, was based on his skillful logic and his record of successful predictions: "Arch is an extremely logical person. He uses clear, analytic progression—there's no leap of faith. He's a very easy guy to follow, especially with his track record"—a comment I heard often from subordinates. As well, it was widely known that he had been the youngest vice-president ever at IBM.

Stage Four: Achieving the Vision. In the final stage, charismatic leaders generally differ from others because of their extensive use of personal example and role modeling, their reliance on unconventional tactics, and their use of empowerment practices to demonstrate how their vision can be achieved. By role modeling certain management practices, by describing their perspectives on the marketplace and their organization, by immersing others in their style of decision making, charismatics convey what they perceive to be the critical approaches to success. As well, their vision may contain elements of an ideology that provides a set of decision rules for day-to-day problem solving and approaches to the market. Moreover, the charismatic leader demonstrates the unconventional tactics the organization must employ if it is to achieve the leader's vision. And through praise charismatics build followers' belief in their ability to achieve the vision.

Returning to Jan Carlzon, we note that his strategy for Scandinavian Airlines was that it be customer-driven. He describes an experience where he, in essence, exemplified that value himself by his actions:

> When I first came to Linjeflyg, I traveled around to various airports. Toward the end of one of these visits, I sensed some uneasiness among the staff but didn't know why. Then one employee tactfully pointed out that they were waiting for me to board the plane. "Is it ready?" I asked. "I didn't hear any announcement." "No, but if you get on now and decide where you want to sit, we can board the rest of the passengers." . . . If you indicate by your actions that you are superior even to your customers, then you can hardly call yourself market oriented. I had just come from the intensely competitive tourist charter business where it was out of the question to take precedence over a passenger. So I waited until everyone else got on board and was

happy there was an extra seat for me. At SAS we pass out magazines and newspapers on the aircraft. We do not always have enough for everyone and sometimes the staff tries to be kind by offering me my pick first. "Out of the question," I tell them. "I cannot take any myself until I know that all the passengers have gotten what they want!" I have heard more than once that the cabin crew interprets these tiny, symbolic gestures in this way: "Even top management is helping give the passengers good service. That shows respect for our jobs." By demonstrating that we ourselves come last after the customers, we are telling our employees—and the customers—what the ranking order really is. [Carlzon, 1987, pp. 94-95]

In essence, Carlzon is demonstrating for employees of SAS that the customer comes first. His actions highlight this value as critical to the success of the airline's strategy. As well, he is modeling the fact that he himself is not superior to others—he is one of them. This tactic is often employed by charismatics and seems to heighten their appeal.

These, in conclusion, are the four stages distinguishing charismatic leaders from others. In the next four chapters we will explore them in detail and see how charismatic leaders develop these abilities and use them so effectively. Before going on, however, I want to mention that all of these types of behavior are interrelated. They constitute a constellation.

A Constellation of Behavior

It would be wrong to assume that the presence of one of the behavioral traits I have described is sufficient to induce perceptions of charisma. Instead, they are, to some extent, dependent on one another. It is this *constellation* of behavior that distinguishes charismatic leaders from other leaders.

In my own research I have come across noncharismatic leaders who had several of the traits associated with charismatic leaders. I know noncharismatics who are gifted visionaries, for example, yet lack other requisite skills. Likewise I am aware of unconventional leaders who are not perceived as charismatic. The difference between these figures and those described as charismatic is the total number, intensity, and relevance of the types of behavior I am describing. At some point, a "critical mass" is achieved and the leader is perceived as charismatic.

The likelihood of subordinates perceiving a leader as charismatic, then, depends on the *number* of charismatic behaviors the leader exhibits, the *intensity* of each behavior expressed by a leader, and the *relevance* of the behavior to the present situation (Conger and Kanungo, 1988a). A leader who is simply unconventional, for instance, is less likely to be perceived as charismatic than one who has a strategic vision, is skilled at articulating his vision, and is unconventional. The more visionary the goals of the leader and the more unconventional the means to achieve them, the greater the likelihood that the leader will be perceived as charismatic.

A leader whose vision fails to incorporate key values of subordinates is unlikely to be perceived as charismatic. And certain types of behavior may be more important sources of charisma in certain organizations than in others. In an organization that is clearly adrift, a strategic vision may become the pivotal attribute to foster charisma. Leaders therefore must understand how relevant their behavior is for their organization. Hence context too plays an important role in affecting this constellation of behavior. While we still have much to learn about charismatic leaders, we can see that they do appear to be distinctively different from other leaders. Their skills in visioning, communicating, building trust, and motivating appear to be exemplary. And when leaders possess the full complement of these skills, the odds are high that they will be perceived as charismatic.

With this basic framework of skills in mind, it is time to examine each one in depth. In the next chapter we begin with visioning. In many ways, this is the most important of all the skills. The other skills are simply means to convey and achieve the vision. Vision, then, is the cornerstone of charismatic leadership.

Chapter 3

Seeing Beyond
Current Realities

Napoleon Bonaparte once said: "Imagination rules the world." By this he meant that those who do not accept current realities but see beyond them become the masters of change. Charismatic leaders appear to possess this quality of imagination. They seem able to sense the shortcomings of this world and then to formulate a dream to overcome them. This unusual ability to foresee strategic opportunities when combined with powerful communication skills is one of the unique features of these leaders.

We will explore these qualities in this chapter and examine how charismatics formulate their visions. As the reader is probably aware, the notion of strategic vision has received considerable attention (see Bennis and Nanus, 1985; Block, 1987; Tichy and Devanna, 1986; Westley and Mintzberg, 1988), so I will not spend much time on the characteristics of vision. There are, however, a number of important questions concerning its source and evolution and whether the visions of charismatic leaders are distinctly different from those of others. As well, there is some debate whether vision is a rational process that can be taught and trained or whether it is a highly complex, unpredictable, and emergent phenomenon that is difficult to replicate, let alone teach. I will attempt to answer these questions, but first we must understand what we mean by strategic vision.

Aspects of Vision

We can think of vision as a mental image conjured up by a leader that portrays a highly desirable future state for the organization. With charismatics, vision often takes on the quality of an ideal or sometimes a far-reaching dream. What makes vision unique in relation to ordinary tactical goals is that it provides a broad perspective on the organization's *purpose.* Unlike tactical goals, which often aim at a greater return on assets or increased market share or the introduction of certain products, vision encompasses abstract goals. Notice how Steven Jobs, the founder of Apple Computer, describes his vision for a new start-up company called Next:

> We wanted to start a company that had a lot to do with education and, in particular, higher education, colleges, and universities. So our vision is that there's a revolution in software going on now on college and university campuses. And it has to do with providing two types of breakthrough software. One is called simulated learning environments. You can't give a student in physics a linear accelerator. You can't give a student in biology a $5 million recombinant DNA laboratory. But you can simulate those things. You can simulate them on a very powerful computer.
>
> It is not possible for students to afford these things. It is not possible for most faculty members to afford these things. So if we can take what we do best, which is to find really great technology and pull it down to a price point that's affordable to people, if we can do the same thing for this type of computer, which is maybe ten times as powerful as a personal computer, that we did for personal computers, then I think we can make a real differ-

ence in the way the learning experience happens in the next five years. And that's what we're trying to do.

... [And] one of my largest wishes is that we build Next from the heart. And the people that are thinking about coming to work for us or buying our products or who want to sell us things feel that—that we're doing this because we have a passion about it. We're doing this because we really care about the higher educational process, not because we want to make a buck, not because, you know, we just want to do it. [Nathan, 1986, pp. 6-7]

Jobs does not describe his company's vision as building *x* number of computers by a certain date or achieving a certain annual growth rate or simply expanding into a particular market. Rather the strategic goal of Next is to *revolutionize* the educational system of a nation. Further, Jobs's vision focuses on a product that does not yet exist, an ideal, a dream. Implicit in Jobs's message is an enormous sense of challenge, which can be distilled as follows: "We are going to create something no one has ever done before. By doing so, we are going to transform the way learning is done in the world. You, as a member of this organization, will be responsible for this fundamental change in society." Jobs is creating goals beyond those of ordinary organizations. Rather than offering rewards of income, titles, or such, he speaks to the employee's desire to make a social contribution. In other words, the vision addresses needs of a higher order and by doing so incorporates the employee's sense of self into the organization's goals. Abraham Maslow (1965) described this state in a similar organizational context: "The task, problem, or purpose was totally introjected by everyone in the situation; that is to say that the task or duty was not any longer something separate from the self, something out there, outside the person and different from him, but rather he identified with this task so strongly that you couldn't define his real self without including the task." For organizational members, then, the vision, in essence, enlarges the frame of their contribution and the worthiness of what they are doing. In turn, it heightens the person's motivational commitment to an organization.

This is not to say that the leader's goals do not also include rewards such as money, fame, or more prestigious positions. The charismatic leader also promises these in return. Mary Kay Ash, the founder of Mary Kay Cosmetics, a highly successful beauty products firm in Dallas, offers her salespeople awards of diamonds, minks, and Cadillacs in great abundance. Thus both higher and lower-order needs are being met by the charismatic's vision and aims. The key difference is that in terms of higher-order needs, the charismatic's message is far more appealing than that of most other leaders.

If we contrast Jobs's description of company's goals with those of a noncharismatic leader I interviewed, we see the difference in terms of the level of appeal: "One of my earlier objectives was to assimilate a collection of smaller breweries into a division and make everything consistent—benefit plans, etc.— which I did. I wanted to upgrade staff, and now we have more professionals. I also wanted to decentralize operations, which is what I've done. The need now is for formal training, better distribution, more optimal routing, better utilization of the distribution system by adding more products, and the purchase of more breweries on the East and West coasts—that would be my grand plan." This executive is concerned with the day-to-day operating goals of his organization and its physical resources. There is no mention of a larger contribution. As well, these goals appear quite within the realm of achievement. There is no idealistic, deeply challenging future state to be achieved. The goals are not inspiring. You, as a reader, can test your own reactions to these two sets of goals. Clearly Jobs has a more visionary and inspiring quality.

Vision as a Strategic Umbrella

Visions, themselves, tend to be surprisingly simple. They are not articulated with an elaborate set of strategic goals and quantitative measurements. They do not focus on detailed business plans or goals and rarely mention market share percentages, revenue targets, or return on investment figures. Rather they begin as a simple idea that provides a "strategic umbrella" under which specific tactics can be worked out as opportunities arise or barriers appear (Mintzberg and Waters, 1985), though the ultimate goal is usually clear. For Jobs, the strategic umbrella of Next is a computer product that will revolutionize education through simulated learning environments. The exact steps to its achievement are not necessarily fully known and instead are determined as the product is developed and brought to market.

In researching vision, I have been consistently surprised at its simplicity. In interviews I would often probe to uncover what I assumed to be a wealth of detail lurking behind initial descriptions of a leader's vision. Yet as I probed, I continued to encounter this sense of simplicity. What I have come to realize is that simplicity is the strength of vision. In essence, the vision serves as an organizing principle or guide for day-to-day decision making within the organization. The vision's goals focus attention on what is important, what is rewarded.

The vision also screens out the unessential for the leader. As one executive told me: "I purposely have a very clear vision. . . . My perception is that there is so much happening, you can't lose yourself in objectives unrelated to the vision." As president of a telecommunications company, he explained that the previous day he had a chance to acquire a company producing residential telephone equipment. Analysis and projections showed it to be an excellent opportunity at a reasonable price. The executive turned it down. It did not mesh with his vision. His own goals were to revolutionize certain sectors of the business communication market, and while there appeared to be opportunities for synergy between the office and home communication markets, he perceived it as a distraction from his principal goal. His vision served not only as a screening device for acquisitions but also for new products and the allocation of financial and human resources. In the case of McGill, his early vision for AT&T was to transform it into a customer-driven organization. Projects that did not further this objective were eliminated.

It can be inferred, then, that vision aids tremendously in

strategic decision making for organizational members. One manager remarked about his leader's vision: "When I'm attending meetings with him, I feel satisfied that there is a conclusion, a clear next step which, from my experience, is unusual with most managers. I think it comes back to having a vision. You need a purpose, you need a focus to chart your course. . . . He looks at current issues in light of the vision. One example. We've had a lot of service measurement indexes in the company tradition. He wants us to reexamine all of them and discard those that don't fit the vision."

Business plans are too lengthy and detailed to accomplish this purpose. People need something simple. Employees focusing on detailed operating plans have a hard time interpreting their organization's overarching goals. A well-articulated strategic vision provides clarity and focus. For example, research on artificial intelligence has shown that people are ineffective at processing large streams of new data and information (Simon, 1979). Most of us can hold in short-term memory, without forgetting, only six or seven pieces of data. The simpler the vision's message, therefore, the greater the likelihood it will be retained.

By providing a few broad concepts rather than a multitude of precise numerical goals, the vision becomes a memory tool allowing many levels of the organization to make decisions without consulting their superiors. As well, a vision provides a set of decision rules that facilitate speed and ensure less frequent errors by subordinates: Does the solution mesh with the vision's goals or not? By minimizing the number of goals, organizational resources can be sharply focused since only a few major strategic goals can be absorbed by an organization at any one time due to resource commitments and ongoing momentum (Quinn, 1980, p. 80).

A powerful counterexample is Robert Sarnoff, the chairman of RCA, who in 1969 attempted to introduce several new strategic thrusts. On the one hand, Sarnoff diversified his company through acquisitions. Simultaneously, he sought to strengthen the company's weak marketing abilities, to move the company's research orientation toward applied technologies, and to strengthen RCA's computer operations so it could compete with IBM. The organization struggled to absorb so much top-level change. The programs encountered serious resistance at the divisional level, the computer project failed, and Sarnoff's credibility was strained (Quinn, 1980, pp. 80–81). This was a case of more strategic goals than the organization could digest.

The initial simplicity with which a vision may arise does not preclude its evolution and transformation. In reality, all visions are bound by time and the leader's concerns, and they may evolve in response to new and unexpected developments. I will describe these dynamics shortly.

Vision as a Stimulus

Apart from providing a clear sense of strategic direction, vision also plays a critical role in motivation. We can appreciate its motivational appeal if we think back to the raison d'être for organizations. Both an organization and the people in it are seeking rewards of some kind. These rewards may be economic or psychosocial—achievement, meaningful work, power, self-esteem, or status. Both parties seek to maximize their rewards—the organization from its position in the marketplace and individuals from their participation in the organization. When the organization has a clear sense of purpose that is widely shared and perceived as meaningful by its members, individuals can then find satisfying roles both in the organization and in society at large. An effective vision integrates into the organization's purpose and into the employee's job a sense of contribution to themselves, to an industry, or to society. This sense of worthiness and influence can lead to greater commitment, enthusiasm, and the motivation to work harder. An effective vision creates for its followers a sense of being at the active centers of a social system—those special arenas in society where change and innovation are taking place (Bennis and Nanus, 1985, p. 82; Eisenstadt, 1968). Employees become empowered by what they perceive as participation in a highly worthwhile enterprise.

Just as important, vision provides a unifying theme for the organization's members. It draws them together as a team, as a community. This sense of teamwork adds to the momentum. One executive familiar with two firms that I had studied described the differences between them: "I saw at Information Dynamics people as a collection of engineers—quiet, stable, conservative, very likeable, but not exciting. Each was doing his thing. At Software Research, I saw a group of individuals with a common vision. A vision that drives the firm. A vision that unites and excites them." Software Research was headed by a highly charismatic leader; Information Dynamics was not.

A Typology of Vision

Most strategic visions can be categorized as one of four types or an amalgamation of several of these types (Figure 2).

Figure 2. A Typology of Visions.

	Narrow Focus	Broad Focus
External Orientation	Product/Service Innovation	Contribution to Society
Internal Orientation	Organizational Transformation	Contribution to the Work Force

Each type is defined by its principal focus—a particular product, the revitalization of an organization, a contribution to society, or a contribution to the work force itself. In reality, of course, the organization's products or services constitute the cornerstone on which the vision is elaborated. Steven Jobs built his vision for Next around a low-priced computer providing simulated learning environments. He then framed, or described, his vision as revolutionizing the educational system through this device. The product is an integral element of the vision. It is the vehicle by which the educational revolution will be achieved. Mary Kay's line of cosmetics is the means through which women in North America will develop confidence and esteem and become, as Mary Kay says, "the beautiful women God intended them to be."

While both Steven Jobs's and Mary Kay's visions speak of broad contributions to society, a vision may be more narrowly defined. A leader many simply describe, for instance, how his or her product will revolutionize their product line without reference to a broad social contribution. But as the frame of the vision widens to include a social or work-force contribution, the likelihood of attributing charisma to a leader may increase. This concept of "framing" a vision is integral to its appeal and is discussed in greater detail in Chapter Four, where we will examine the manner in which the vision is articulated and communicated. Briefly, the four types of vision are:

- *Visions with a Product/Service Focus:* The strategic goal here is to create a new product or service. It is an externally focused vision in that employees derive their satisfaction from a contribution toward transforming the nature of a particular product and its marketplace. Examples of this type include Edwin Land's vision of instant photography or John DeLorean, the General Motors executive who attempted to create his own sports car. The vision is narrowly defined in terms of introducing a product that will either have lasting appeal or revolutionize the marketplace.
- *Visions with a Transformational Focus:* Here the strategic goal is to transform a deeply troubled organization into a viable entity. Lee Iacocca's vision for Chrysler and Bob Lipp's for Chemical Bank best exemplify this strategic aim. The vision is intended to restore the health of the organization. Although its focus is essentially inward, it necessarily involves changes in the company's products and services.
- *Visions with a Social Focus:* In this category the strategic aim is to transform certain aspects of society through the com-

pany's products or services. Steven Jobs's aim at Next, for example, is not simply to create a revolutionary new product but to transform the process of learning in society. Arch McGill's vision was not simply to introduce revolutionary new AT&T products but to restore productivity to American industry through the savings his company's products would generate for their users.

Visions with an Employee Focus: Here the products or services are secondary in the sense that they are only a means of making organizational life more meaningful for employees. Mary Kay speaks of her mission not as selling more cosmetics but as making her women employees "all they can be." The company represents a path to personal growth. Donald Burr, founder of People Express, described his airline's mission: "I guess the single predominant reason that I cared about starting a new company was to try and develop a better way for people to work together. . . . That's where the name People Express came from [as well as the] whole people focus and thrust. . . . It drives everything else we do." The airline in his vision then became the means for creating an organization that met the human needs of its employees.

In reality, visions often overlap on these dimensions. Donald Burr's vision for People Express incorporated both an employee contribution and a service innovation as the airline attempted to become the first "Trailways" of the air travel industry with its low-cost airfare. Mary Kay implicitly recognizes a social contribution by making women in general into more fully functioning members of the business community and by bolstering women's confidence in their own abilities. As well, leaders may enlarge the focus of their vision as they come to see the broad ramifications of their product or service. Edwin Land later spoke of his instant cameras as not simply a revolution in photography but a new step in building closer relationships in society. Bob Lipp began with a vision of revitalizing Chemical Bank's retail operations; after accomplishing this goal, he went on to develop a vision of home banking services (see Chapter Eight). This progression is probably a common occurrence as leaders accomplish one set of goals and then turn their sights on others. New visions may emerge as old ones are achieved.

Charismatic versus Noncharismatic Visions

Strategic vision is not the exclusive property of charismatic leaders—it is probably essential for most entrepreneurs whether charismatic or not. In mature organizations, however, it is probably a rare trait among noncharismatic leaders. In either case, a leader is more likely to be perceived as charismatic if the vision takes on certain qualities. The more idealized the goals of the leader, for example, the more likely they will be seen as charismatic (as long as they are believed attainable). After he became president of AT&T's Advanced Information Systems division, Arch McGill described his organization's goal not as increased market share but as restoring American productivity through the division's advances in electronic technology. His division was not simply seeking to develop and market advanced telecommunication devices; it was trying to achieve the lofty ideal of revitalizing North America's sagging industry. He would say to his staff in a full-page newspaper advertisement:

> As of today, our number-one priority is to help give American business a much needed shot in the arm. . . . For some . . . the American dream is in question. The single most important key to the resurgence of that dream, to its viability . . . and the building of a positive vision of the future . . . is an innovative, vibrant, growing, and highly productive business community. What greater challenge is there? We have the talent, the skills, and the commitment to help America once again assert its preeminent position in the world economy. . . . Our customers must know what they can expect from us . . . what they can depend on us for: (1) an undaunted commitment to marketplace needs, (2) an undaunted commitment to the search for excellence, and (3) an undaunted commitment from

you. That kind of commitment is what it's going to take from us to survive in the competitive arena. It will mean acting, on your own initiative, without hesitation . . . calling on all of your talents, skills, creativity, and savvy . . . whenever and wherever it's required. . . . I am excited about what the future holds. . . . Now let's get on with it.

Contrast this announcement with a noncharismatic leader's description of his vision for a food products company: "I would have to say that it's consumer value in consumer packaged goods—value in terms of price, quality, and relationship with the customer." He himself admitted that "I don't get a lot of my staff jumping in on it. . . . It's an abstraction—a little hard to relate to." In interviews, his subordinates agreed. Instead of presenting an inspiring ideal, this leader describes a mundane goal. When probed further about his strategic aims, he described his plans to expand the company's product line through acquisitions into household goods such as cleansers. Through such products, he would build on the company's strength in supermarket distribution. Again, however, there is no element of a particularly challenging future. This leader's goals are simply an incremental extension of the company's present strategy. They are not a radical departure.

Related to ideals, then, is the notion that the more the leader's goals challenge the present situation, the more likely subordinates are to attribute to him an extraordinary vision. This attribution of extraordinariness is a crucial ingredient in perceptions of charisma. Steven Jobs's vision, for example, represents a monumental departure from present-day reality. He is portraying a world in which students can simulate on their own computers the processes of a multi-million-dollar linear accelerator. This possibility heightens the extraordinariness of the mission of Next. As an ideal, the vision conveys a tremendous sense of challenge.

We might also hypothesize that the greater the degree to which the vision is shared by employees and addresses their deepest aspirations, the greater the likelihood the leader will be seen as charismatic. The perceived potential of the leader to fulfill these needs creates the basis for an attraction to the leader, along with the perception that the leader shares similar values and beliefs. Take Bob Lipp and Mary Kay Ash, for example. Lipp's turnaround program with its bank "president" concept, described in the previous chapter, specifically addressed his employees' need to feel important and special. Mary Kay Ash, when she founded Mary Kay Cosmetics in 1963, created the vision of her firm not so much around her cosmetics but around the need her organization would fulfill for many women in the 1960s and 1970s. Specifically, she described her company's mission as guided by God himself with the aim of helping women live more fulfilled lives.

Her vision then pitched itself toward meeting the diverse needs of modern women. The timing was exquisite. In the 1960s and 1970s, the women's liberation movement had begun its attempts at transforming the roles that women had played historically as housewives and second-class citizens. Mary Kay offered a career for these women—one that uniquely fit their emerging needs. It met their needs for financial freedom, for instance, giving a housewife a source of income outside her husband's. Her career could also be pursued at home where the cosmetics sales were transacted. Thus the woman consultant could be with her children and manage her own day independently as she had done as a housewife, yet still be a successful businessperson. This excerpt from a brochure targeted to new consultants captures the essence of this appeal: "You can add another dimension to your life, and add to your income, while taking nothing away from all the other people you are. Many [Mary Kay] beauty consultants are wives and mothers. As independent businesswomen, they can choose their own hours and easily schedule their Mary Kay activities to fit a schedule that puts family first."

Finally, Mary Kay and her organization spent an inordinate amount of time building the egos of her consultants. She lauded them in public meetings. She rewarded them with jewelry,

furs, and pink Cadillacs. She provided them with praise and rewards, therefore, that were generally absent from their lives.
Mary Kay's vision uniquely fulfilled the unmet needs of an
emerging work force of women.

Formulation of the Vision

Strategic vision, on the surface, appears deceptively simple. It can be articulated in a few lines and is more often a general statement of mission than an intricate set of strategic goals.
Its formulation, however, is usually the product of a complex
set of forces. Contrary to recent descriptions of "visioning" as a
rational step-by-step process (Block, 1987; Sashkin, 1988; Tichy
and Devanna, 1986), it is significantly more complex. In reality,
it is the product of the leader's personal experiences and abilities in combination with a set of opportunities.

Of the charismatic leaders whose biographies I have studied, there are certain patterns that characterize the roots of
their vision. Sometimes it begins in childhood with a particular
set of interests and drives that are then crystallized during their
career years by personal experiences, insights, and opportunities. Serendipity and timing also play an important part. I can
illustrate one of the pathways by which vision is formulated by
describing a representative example: Donald Burr, founder of
People Express airline (Rhodes, 1984; Whitestone, 1983).

In the 1980s, Donald Burr founded a new airline that
achieved phenomenal success for several years. His strategic vision involved tapping the low-price end of the airline market—a
strategy that had met with only moderate success in the past.
Beginning with two hundred and fifty employees in 1980, his
company, People Express, grew to three thousand full and part-
time employees within two and a half years. By 1986, People
Express had reached revenues of $1.2 billion. As *Inc.* magazine
stated: "By all accounts, People Express is, quite simply, the
fastest-growing airline in the history of aviation" (Rhodes, 1984,
p. 42).

Burr's product was essentially a seat on an aircraft flying
between Newark, New Jersey, and another major city on the

East Coast that was, most of all, cheap. A typical commercial airline fare between New York and Boston during the mid-1980s, for example, was $57 during peak hours and $42 off peak. The People Express shuttle offered twenty flights a day between New York and Boston for $38 peak and $25 off peak. In return for these reduced fares, passengers paid extra for services that were normally included in the airline fare such as baggage checking and snacks and drinks on board.

The success of this strategy can be seen in the airline's "load factor"—the actual portion of seats filled by paying customers. Throughout the 1980s, the airline industry's average load factor was 60 percent; by mid-1983 People Express had reached a remarkable 83.6 percent. How did Donald Burr develop the vision to see a market opportunity that others did not? What were the essential ingredients of his insight?

His vision begins in childhood where he first fell in love with airplanes. He once described how he would badger his parents into driving him to the neighborhood airport to watch the airplanes every Sunday. He also had an early interest in business. He describes his experience with the local candy store: "I used to go into the candy store and wonder how that guy ran that store. I thought I could never do that—run a store, order all those things. Kids would talk about Mickey Mantle hitting home runs. I thought that was great how that guy ran that store. I've always been like that. I've always wanted to know how you put those things together" (Rhodes, 1984, p. 44). Early in his life, then, we see interests that would develop into Burr's career path in entrepreneurship in the airline industry.

After graduation from Harvard Business School with an MBA, Burr pursued his interest in aviation by joining the National Aviation Corporation as a securities analyst. The company specialized in airlines and aerospace securities and venture capital. Within six years, he was elected company president and, by age thirty-one, was already an expert in the financial strategies and economics of launching and running an airline. This period of time as an analyst provided Burr with a broad exposure to the industry and all aspects of the business.

Soon afterward, Burr was approached by Houston-based

Texas International Airlines, a regional carrier that had a long history of mismanagement and was in financial trouble. They asked Burr to help turn the airline around. From his experience as a securities analyst, he recalled that in the early 1960s a California airline, Pacific Southwest, had used low-price fares as a marketing strategy to increase traffic. Faced with a similar problem, Burr decided to test this same strategy. The idea, then, was not really Burr's but based on the experience of others. Burr introduced the new fare strategy under the name of "Mr. Peanut," which became the symbol for Texas International's new low-cost "peanut fares." The plan worked. Air traffic and profits rose, and in 1976 Burr was made the company's chief operating officer. By 1979, he was appointed president.

What we see in this case is a visionary leader drawing upon ideas and tactics he may have come upon in earlier work experiences. He may have seen similar strategies succeed, though perhaps on a smaller scale or in a different context. He may be able to see parallels between approaches in another industry that would be innovative in his own. He then incorporates these ideas into his vision. In this case, Burr's experience with Texas International provided the training ground for experimentation and the initial ideas for the People Express strategy. (This is not what I have discovered in interviews with inventor-entrepreneurs who go on to become charismatic leaders of their organizations, however. In their case, either individually or as part of a team, they may have discovered the initial product idea that became the company's strategic vision.)

For reasons that are not entirely clear, Burr departed from Texas International six months after his appointment as president. Initially he had no clear direction in mind. Significantly, however, a historic event had occurred the year before: The U.S. Congress passed the Airline Deregulation Act of 1978 that allowed airlines to compete aggressively in both route selection and pricing; it also encouraged new entrants to the market. A unique opportunity presented itself—the end of forty years of airline regulation. It was a moment of serendipity for Burr. Sensing a historic moment at exactly the same time he was searching for a new challenge, Burr began to contemplate starting a new airline. The next element of vision now appears: A unique market opportunity presents itself and the visionary leader is able to sense the uniqueness of the moment.

In April 1980, Burr incorporated People Express—whose name, as Burr described it, reflected his own concern that companies needed to focus on their most important asset, their people. Burr himself had experienced a growing dissatisfaction with what he perceived as commonplace corporate attitudes toward employees. He explained: "Most organizations frustrate people who really want to work. They control them, and watch them, and check up on them. They subsume the individual. They consider them guilty until proven innocent" (Rhodes, 1984, p. 45). He told Harvard Business School case writers: "I cared about starting a new company . . . to try and develop a better way for people to work together" (Whitestone, 1983, p. 5). This emphasis on an organization driven by people-sensitive policies then became an essential part of the vision, manifesting itself in tactical decisions such as an employee stock plan, extensive job rotation, freedom from seniority regulations.

This characteristic is common to some charismatic leaders. They formulate into their visions a set of personal values that are idealistic—in this case, providing a humanistic work environment. These values reflect a sensitivity to employee and marketplace needs. In Burr's case, the sensitivity to people's concerns comes directly from his own experience as a dissatisfied employee in prior jobs. We find the same situation, though more painfully experienced, with charismatic political and religious leaders such as Gandhi and Martin Luther King who both experienced a discrimination early in their lives that caused them to become hypersensitive to their followers' needs. These leaders did not have to guess what their constituents were feeling; they knew from firsthand experience. This may explain the empathy certain charismatic leaders show toward their followers.

Three events, then, were critical in crystallizing the ideas of Burr's strategic vision into a reality. The first opportunity was a lunch with Bill Hambrecht of Hambrecht & Quist, one of the nation's foremost new-venture investment firms. This encounter ultimately led to Hambrecht's underwriting an equity issue of $24 million for People Express. The second opportunity was the availability of terminal space close to a high-density urban population and with central access to East Coast cities—the Newark, New Jersey, airport. It provided strategic access to New York City and northern New Jersey—two vast markets. The final and serendipitous factor was Burr's discovery in a trade journal that Lufthansa, the German airline, was selling a fleet of twenty-two used Boeing 737s. People Express negotiated for seventeen of the planes for approximately $70 million—the equivalent of $4.1 million per aircraft as compared to $13 million for a new 737. These three tactical opportunities were essential to the ultimate realization of Burr's vision. They were factors, especially the latter two, that simply presented themselves at the right moment. Whether People Express would have ultimately succeeded without them is a good question.

From Burr's history we see that strategic vision is very much an incremental process spurred on by past experiences, creative insights, opportunism, and serendipity. We can also think of strategic vision as involving several distinct but incremental stages or experiences, each contributing to a broad understanding of the marketplace:

- Early adulthood or early to mid-career interests
- Broad exposure to product service and industry during early career
- Exposure to innovative ideas and tactics
- Personal experiences that heighten sensitivity to constituents and marketplace needs
- Period of experimentation with innovative ideas and tactics
- Appearance of market/technology opportunities

A leader may not have to pass through all the stages or experiences outlined here for a vision to arise, but many of them are essential steps leading to a successful vision. They do not occur necessarily in a linear fashion but may be more recursive. Later stages may impact earlier ones, and vice versa. Let us now look at why each might make an important contribution to the process.

Childhood or Early Adulthood Interest. Especially with respect to inventors who become entrepreneurs, an early interest in a technology or product may be important for their development. I say this because it seems imperative that the person have a comprehensive understanding of the technical fundamentals to succeed. This comes about often after years of education and experience with the subject.

At times, a leader's vision may represent a passionate interest. This passion may start early on in life. We certainly see this with Donald Burr and his childhood love of airplanes. Lee Iacocca in his autobiography mentions a decision at age fifteen to go into the automobile industry. John DeLorean's love affair with cars began with his birth in America's motor city, Detroit. His father worked at Ford, and John supposedly began tinkering with cars by age ten (Levin, 1983). In high school, Steven Jobs made a living buying, selling, and trading electronic equipment. He became intensely interested in video equipment and computers shortly afterward. Two of the charismatic leaders that I studied developed their interest in computer software and data processing during college days. Both would go on to found their own firms.

This interest in a product or service leads the individual, I would argue, to a greater understanding of its market and its untapped uses. These leaders simply enjoy exploring opportunities or new ways to approach problems relevant to their interest. There are numerous exceptions to this pattern, though. Mary Kay Ash, for example, was not involved in the cosmetics industry at an early age nor were any members of her family. She was, however, attracted to jobs involving selling. And her long-time belief in looking feminine and attractive embodied itself in her company's ideology. Bob Lipp and several of the other executives I studied developed interests in what were to become their visions only after graduation from college and some work experience; nonetheless they all began these interests at a fairly early stage—at the very latest, by mid-career.

Broad Exposure to a Product/Service and Industry During Early Career. Returning to the example of Donald Burr, we see that after graduation from Harvard he assumed a position as an airline industry analyst that allowed him to see the industry from a broad perspective. He also learned about competitive tactics such as low-cost fares and financing schemes. This early exposure to a market or product provides the future leader with a unique vantage point from which to see emerging trends and therefore opportunities that others might not detect.

John DeLorean, for example, chose to start his career at the Packard Motor Car Company. Unlike the Big Three, this small car company afforded a breadth of experience the larger ones did not: "I've always had to see how and what I did integrated with the whole. That was not obvious to me in a large company," remarked DeLorean about Packard (Levin, 1983, p. 28). The company was too small to afford many specialists, so engineers had to be generalists. Engineers also had the freedom to experiment with designs and equipment. Unlike the larger manufacturers, Packard let DeLorean follow a design from the drafting board to its implementation on the factory floor (p. 30). Through this early experience, he was able to gain a breadth of exposure to the car-making process that few in the industry at his age would have possessed—later laying the groundwork for his own car company. McGill had a similarly broad range of experience in computers and telecommunications. The two data systems executives that I studied were involved in a wide range of EDS projects during their early career years. There are exceptions, of course. Lipp, for instance, had no experience as a bank branch manager; he did, however, have a breadth of experience in bank management and financial control systems. Though it may be possible for certain leaders to be visionary without such breadth and depth, I suspect that they are exceptions.

Broad exposure to a market or product early in one's career, then, probably provides two advantages. First, the person is able to develop a comprehensive understanding of an industry or product and, as a result, is in a much better position to detect shortcomings and emerging opportunities. Second, because of this broad exposure he or she is in a stronger position to manage the multiple functional aspects associated with a particular product or service. Interestingly, the noncharismatic leaders in my 1985 study were functional specialists—principally finance and marketing—until their middle or later career years.

So Burr understood airlines, Jobs computers, McGill communications. Mary Kay Ash had extensive selling experience. Iaccoca spent his lifetime in the automobile industry. These are not figures who shifted from expertise to expertise. Rather they had a depth of experience that allowed them to see opportunities as well as shortcomings in their respective markets. They had intimate connections with the products and services of their organizations, though they may not always have been the originating genius. Vision, then, depends in part on a depth of knowledge of one's product and markets. This was certainly the case with all the charismatic leaders I have interviewed. The implications for training are obvious. Educational programs or workshops that attempt to teach vision skills to managers with only limited experience in their industries are not likely to be successful.

Exposure to Innovative Ideas and Tactics. Most visionary leaders were exposed to original and innovative ideas during their careers. A popular myth holds that the charismatic leader is always the originator of these ideas. Occasionally, and more so with inventor-entrepreneurs, these ideas do originate with the leader, but the charismatic may just as often borrow from the experiences and ideas of others or develop them jointly with others. Charismatic leaders can be in many ways exceptional *promoters* of an idea if not always its originator.

From Burr's history we can see that the initial ideas for a low-cost airline came from his knowledge of Pacific Southwest and then his experimentation with this idea at Texas International. Mary Kay Ash is credited with pioneering the home "party" for selling cosmetics; in reality, the idea came from her experiences as a salesperson for Stanley Home Products. Stanley sold housecleaning products directly to its customers through "house parties." They also employed a particular motivational device—an annual sales conference in Dallas. At the convention, the top saleswoman was awarded a "Queen of Sales" title and crowned in front of the other sales representatives. Mary Kay Ash herself was so motivated by the experience that she approached company president F. Stanley Beveridge and promised that she would be the next year's queen. "He took my hand in both of his, looked me square in the eye, and after a moment said solemnly: 'Somehow I think you will.' These five words changed my life.'' By the next year, she had accomplished her goal. From this experience she would later develop an annual sales conference for her own company where top salespeople would be crowned as queens and publicly rewarded with words of encouragement just as Beveridge had done. She would also define her principal role as praising and motivating her salespeople as Beveridge had done for her.

When John DeLorean left Packard to join the Pontiac division of General Motors, his new boss was Semon "Bunkie" Knudsen, known as the company miracle-worker for his turnarounds of GM's tank division, the Allison aircraft engine division, and Cleveland Diesel. He was also a great lover of sports cars. Bill Collins, an engineer at Pontiac who later joined DeLorean's car company, described the atmosphere of Pontiac at the time: "From an engineer's standpoint, the late fifties and early sixties at Pontiac were some of the most exciting years in the history of GM. We seemed to constantly be on the cutting edge of product innovation" (Levin, 1983, p. 35). Knudsen was particularly sensitive to styling. During DeLorean's tenure as chief engineer and general manager of Pontiac, the division would be responsible for styling innovations such as recessed windshield wipers, hidden radio antennas, racing stripes, squared-off headlights, and endura bumpers (p. 44). From these experiences, DeLorean would begin to mold his ideas for creating a stylish sports car that would become the centerpiece of DeLorean's own automobile company. Its distinctive features would include a pair of gull-wing doors that swung open over the car's roof, a stainless steel body, a driver's cockpit equipped with airbags, and bumpers that could withstand an impact of ten miles an hour without damage. (The industry standard was three miles an hour at the time.) These ideas were all borrowed. After World War II, Mercedes-Benz used gull-wings for racing cars to cut down on wind resistance; in 1956, they even built a commercial production model, the Mercedes 300SL. And as far back as 1936, a stainless steel manufacturer, Allegheny-Ludlum, redesigned a Ford car with a stainless steel body for demonstration purposes. It would never rust and never need paint—a revolutionary idea. Similar to studies of Lee Iacocca's vision of the Mustang, we find DeLorean's vision more the product of a number of individuals' ideas than the creation of one person's mind.

This is also the case with Steven Jobs. Much of the technical success of Apple Computer can be attributed to Stephen Wozniak (better known as "The Woz"), a friend of Steven Jobs. Wozniak essentially designed the Apple I and II personal computers. It was Jobs who orchestrated the organization to produce and market these products. Jobs knew also how to get investors and supporters for these products. Regis McKenna, who designed advertising for the semiconductor giants of the time, captured Jobs's distinct competence: "I don't deny that Woz designed a good machine. But that machine would be sitting in hobby shops today were it not for Steven Jobs. Woz was fortunate to hook up with an evangelist" (Freiberger and Swaine, 1984, p. 219). A similar situation occurred with Apple's second innovation—the Macintosh computer. Its easy-to-use computer language, the outstanding graphics, and the "mouse" device were all originally development projects of the Xerox Corporation. Jobs had made two trips to their Palo Alto research center (PARC) where he witnessed the new language "Smalltalk," which emphasized graphics and the mouse—a control device that allows users to select options by pointing at objects on the screen. He then returned to Apple, hired one of PARC's principal scientists, and pushed for development of the Macintosh incorporating these features.

From experiences with the banking industry, which uses centralized clearinghouses for checks, Fred Smith, chairman of Federal Express (the overnight delivery service company), "borrowed" the idea of using a central airport hub (in Tennessee) as a clearinghouse for his packages from around the nation. Several of Arch McGill's later ideas were derived from research projects of his staff. Similar sources of ideas were used by charismatic leaders in other mature organizations I have studied. For example, a new technology or market research finding might be presented to the leader. He, in turn, would recognize its broader implications. These leaders seem to be very skillful at seeing innovative ideas and then incorporating them into their vision either as the focal point, such as a product like the Macintosh, or as a tactic such as Mary Kay Ash's home selling parties. The charismatic leader, in essence, can be a very effective promoter of ideas, not necessarily the inventor of those ideas. This is particularly true of charismatic leaders who are not inventors of the original product or service themselves.

Personal Experiences That Heighten Sensitivity to Constituents' Needs and Market Demands. Many charismatic leaders appear to have had personal experiences that made them more sensitive to their constituents' needs and market demands. We saw how Donald Burr's dissatisfaction as an employee led him to devise a more humanistic structure for People Express. Mary Kay Ash's father was an invalid. She worked as the family housekeeper while her mother worked to support the family financially. In later life, she would marry, have three children, and divorce. Out of financial need, the divorce would force her into work as a salesperson for Stanley Home Products. Her early experiences were of women struggling to achieve financial independence while striving to be supportive of their family. She had quite painfully experienced what many of the increasingly liberated women of the 1960s would experience. Steven Jobs's network of friends were computer hackers from Silicon Valley. He knew their interests and what motivated them. At one of my research sites, the head of manufacturing for a computer company had fifteen years of plant start-up experience before he became the charismatic leader of his organization. He knew firsthand what the problems and experiences of his subordinates would be as they attempted to expand operations dramatically by opening numerous new plants.

From a market standpoint, it also appears that a number of the visionary leaders had early experiences that put them directly in touch with market demands. John DeLorean helped with Pontiac's entry into the small-car market—the Pontiac Tempest. Using components General Motors had already produced, he blended them into a new car that became the division's best-selling product. He would later do the same thing with many of the internal components of his own sports car. He would discover that often the market cared more about styling than engineering. In 1962, he and another manager had promoted a "clean look" car called the Grand Prix to corporate headquarters. Denied additional tooling funds, they were forced to use an existing body. Removing most of the exterior chrome and adding more elegant interior appointments, they produced the "new" Grand Prix. The car sold out in its first run of 40,000.

Ross Perot, the charismatic and legendary founder of Electronic Data Systems (EDS), built a remarkably successful data processing company. He began his career as a salesman for IBM. From this experience in selling the line of IBM computer hardware, he observed that many of his customers could not use their computers effectively. He began to formulate the idea of providing data processing services with hardware to meet these needs. He would then leave IBM and found EDS, which grew from nothing in 1962 to $4.3 billion by 1986. The data systems company presidents in my own studies had extensive experience in implementing such systems and knew intimately the dilemmas their clients faced. Such experiences bring leaders in touch with their constituents' needs.

Period of Experimentation with Ideas and Tactics. It would be wrong to think that somehow, quite miraculously, the leader's vision simply appears one day. The process is much more gradual. Donald Burr first experimented with the strategy of a low-price fare at Texas International; only much later would the complete vision of People Express materialize.

Visions tend to be in constant evolution because of new experiences and their trials in the marketplace and in their organizations. The leader may experiment with the initial ideas to test their possibilities and the receptivity of the organization and marketplace. As they succeed or are accepted, new insights about the market and constituents may cause the vision to develop its conceptual quality, its appeal to higher values. As well, a leader may achieve his vision and then turn to another one as in the case of Steven Jobs and Bob Lipp.

Arch McGill's visions illustrate this evolutionary process. His original mandate was to aid AT&T in the effort to become more market-driven. His vision at this point was simply to provide market research that would reveal, through facts, the serious inconsistencies in AT&T's perceptions of its market. He then developed what he called a "customer-driven" vision where all activity was directed to understanding and addressing marketplace needs. But fairly early on, he also began to perceive a far more significant role for communications than had traditionally been recognized. He saw that technology was on the verge of creating information markets. By the mid-1970s, he sensed that the new communication technologies would no longer reside in the telephone networks themselves but in the offices of users. His experience in computer technology and market research pointed to a sense that information technologies would play an astonishing role in industry. By 1980, he was appointed vice-president of marketing. In this position he conducted a series of large-scale research projects that would bring his various market insights together into a more "conceptually evolved" and appealing vision. The research studies revealed a remarkable role for communications. An executive on the team explained: "We looked at how different industries made decisions, how they processed information, and we studied and measured all aspects of what the communications process was. We came up with the astonishing fact that 50 percent of U.S. industry's total operating costs were in communications, excluding interest expense and raw materials. The premise was that if we understood how much it really costs to communicate, then we could look for alternatives. Salary expense was 84 percent of that communications expense; very little was covered by technology. There was an enormous opportunity for electronic technology—teleconferencing and electronic mail—and, perhaps more importantly, productivity improvements. Arch said, 'This is a concept! Let's tell everyone it's not their job to sell telecommunications but to make American industry productive.'" What we see here is a stream of experiences and insights, one building on the other, ultimately producing a more evolved vision.

Market, Resource, and Technological Opportunities. One important element of vision is sometimes beyond the direct control of the visionary leader—the market, technological, or even resource opportunities that may present themselves. The leader perceives these opportunities and seizes them. In Donald Burr's history, we certainly see this with the appearance of the Airline Deregulation Act, the availability of the New Jersey terminal, and Lufthansa's heavily discounted jets. As well, the equities markets were ripe for a public offering of People Express stock. They were enjoying a heyday at the time for new issues of start-up companies. Burr was not responsible for these factors; what he was responsible for was taking advantage of the opportunities they presented and in turn creating his airline.

In 1963, Mary Kay Ash resigned from her second employer, the World Gift Company, over a policy dispute. She had decided to write a book about her business experiences at the time, but along the way she became intrigued by the idea of starting her own company. She began searching for a product that was "easy to demonstrate and sell, and like Stanley's cleaners and polishes, used 'up' in the process of being used so that her salespeople could establish ongoing relationships with the customers" (Stengrevics, 1981, p. 6). In other words, she was looking for a company and product building on her experience. At that time, she knew of a woman who had developed a skin conditioner but had failed in marketing the product. Mary Kay Ash thought the product was sound; its failure was more the result of poor management skills. For Mary Kay Ash, the opportunity simply presented itself. This product would become the initial offering of Mary Kay Cosmetics.

Shortly after he stepped down from Apple Computer, Steven Jobs contemplated the possibility of new ventures. He spent days reading books on science in search of ideas. He had been reading microbiology texts and became intrigued by DNA and how it replicated itself. He phoned Paul Berg, a Nobel prize winner in biochemistry at Stanford, and over a 2½-hour lunch, Berg explained the recombination of DNA in the laboratory and how it was a time-consuming process of trial and error. Jobs was curious whether Berg had ever attempted to speed up these experiments by simulating them on a computer. Berg had, but the computer hardware to manage such complex simulations was extremely expensive and the existing software was primitive. With a burst of enthusiasm, Jobs exclaimed that he wanted to start a new computer company and that this might just be the product. For Jobs, this meeting would open the door to his next opportunity: the Next computer company. Remember as well that Jobs continued to build upon his prior experience in personal computers and that the new vision of Next would in essence be an extension of an earlier vision of revolutionizing education through the personal computer as he had done at Apple.

Demystifying Vision

From a process standpoint, the formulation of strategic vision is best described by management researcher James Quinn: "The processes used to arrive at the total strategy are typically fragmented, evolutionary, and largely intuitive. . . . The real strategy tends to evolve as internal decisions and external events flow together. . . . The rationale behind this kind of incremental strategy formulation is so powerful that it—rather than step-by-step formal systems planning approach so often espoused—probably provides the best normative model for strategic decision making" (Quinn, 1980, p. 15).

Once the initial direction is in place, the leader is essentially involved in a constant process of collecting relevant information from multiple perspectives. At the same time, he or she is employing conceptual skills to create a gestalt of emerging opportunities or shortcomings that a product might fulfill. While the leader may have an endpoint in mind, the evolution to that point is opportunistic. Fred Smith, CEO of Federal Express, describes his process of developing a vision for his organization: "Pogo, the cartoon character, pointed out one time that the way to be a great leader is to see a parade and run like hell to get in front of it. And there's a lot of truth to that. I don't know of many innovations where somebody sort of just dreamed up an idea out of the clear blue and went off. I mean, there are usually some fairly discernable trends available for a long time indicating a demand for a product or a service. And the time to act on that—to get to the front of the parade, if you will—is when that demand, and the technology needed to meet it, begin to converge" (Tucker, 1986, p. 35).

When asked the sources of his vision, Smith described a process of analyzing them from multiple perspectives: "The key is to be constantly subjecting problems to every possible angle of scrutiny that you can think of, with the idea that, unless you're trying to defy the laws of nature, you'll find some way to solve that problem" (p. 37). I witnessed this same process among my own research subjects. The charismatic leaders were great information collectors with a difference—they used multiple and often apparently unrelated sources of information. Fred Smith says: "Mostly, I think it is the ability to assimilate information from a lot of different disciplines all at once, particularly information about change, because from change comes opportunity. So you might be reading something about the cultural history of the United States, and come to some realization about where the country is headed demographically. The common trait of people who supposedly have vision is that they spend a lot of time reading and gathering information, and then synthesize it until they come up with an idea" (p. 48). One charismatic executive that I studied so personified this stereotype that he would awake at 3:00 A.M. and read a wide range of books until 6:30 A.M. when his day started. We often discussed his interests in philosophy, oriental art, and spirituality while talking about business issues. Colleagues would say, "You'll be constantly amazed by his breadth of knowledge."

What appears to be intuition, then, is really an ability to synthesize diverse information, weeding out the irrelevant, and then conceptualizing it into a coherent picture. It is essentially a creative process. We know from research on creativity that immersion in a particular problem and careful reasoning are more common pathways to creativity than the "creative spark." Creativity is governed more by purpose than process—with purpose serving as the organizing force between the many diverse sources of information and insight that a creative person may generate. The charismatic leader sets out with a clear though global purpose. Jobs wants to create a low-cost computer system that can reproduce simulated learning environments; the process of achieving that goal involves a series of unfolding events and opportunities.

Innovation also appears to be more often the result of a

person's attempts at doing something difficult rather than something original: "Unreasonable demands often force invention, by excluding conventional solutions and requiring the maker to search beyond them" (Perkins, 1981, p. 100). And while chance may from time to time play a role, it favors the prepared mind. We saw a similar dynamic with Donald Burr and Mary Kay Ash. For this reason, we do not find business executives discovering new antibodies or physicists designing automobiles. Creativity reflects the accomplishments of individuals who have committed themselves to a particular task or industry and, as a result, possess the frame of mind to take informative accidents as significant. The ends govern the means, though the ends may be quite broad in their early stages: "Intents to create or to satisfy unreasonable demands, or both, pattern and bias those component processes toward creative accomplishment" (p. 101).

The second element of vision involves risk. Launching a new product or service or, for that matter, an entire computer company or airline involves a measure of risk, sometimes extreme risk. At this point, I suspect that only leaders prepared to assume such risks enter the process. The leader must therefore be risk-oriented or simply less sensitive to risk. Timing and serendipity are also critical elements in whether the strategic vision will ultimately materialize into success. Certainly these two elements were critical for People Express's initial takeoff. Fred Smith shares a similar reaction: "Very important—knowing when to really go and when to sit on the sidelines. Once you decide to go, certainly serendipity plays a big part in it. But I think timing is more important than luck. In my case, for example, the idea that is Federal Express absolutely, positively, would not have worked five years before we did it for many reasons. And five years later, the market would have been so clear that somebody would have served it in one way or another" (Tucker, 1986, p. 49). This window of opportunity is perhaps most narrow for technologies because of their rapid change; other industries might have more latitude.

These, then, are some of the basic forces behind the strategic visions of charismatic leaders. We see that strategic vision when articulated is surprisingly simple; yet when we examine the evolution of a specific leader's vision it appears to be a much more complex process. Events stretching as far back as childhood may influence its origins. As well, it requires a special sensitivity to market forces and constituents' needs. Ultimately, however, its success may lie beyond the leader's abilities, for timing, the right opportunity, and luck can determine whether the vision will be realized or not. With these insights into the cornerstone of charismatic leadership, we next turn our attention to how charismatic leaders breathe life into their vision by the way they communicate its message. Simply having a vision is itself insufficient to motivate and inspire a work force. It is the words chosen to describe the vision and the manner of communicating that give the vision its power.

Chapter 4

Communicating a Vision That Inspires

Mark Twain once exclaimed: "Lord, what an organ is human speech when played on by a master." He was referring to the power of speech to move people emotionally. He knew from experience that speech could transform people's moods and attitudes. A similar understanding is needed by today's business leaders. Persuading through the spoken word can be a far more potent force for change than orders or dictates. With the advent of a better-educated work force, employment laws, and the concept of the democratic workplace, most executives find it difficult simply to dictate their wishes. Because employees must often be *persuaded* to commit to a course of action, a manager's ability to communicate has become more critical. Yet ironically the use of language to influence others has been largely overlooked in management research.

This neglect is surprising since, outside of the written word, speech is our primary means of communication. There is little question that a skillful speaker—whether an evangelist, politician, or actor—can captivate us, persuade us, and spur us to action. The charismatic business leader is no exception.

This ability to communicate and persuade—especially on

an emotional level—is an important feature of the charismatic leader and one of the stages of our model. In field studies comparing charismatic to noncharismatic leaders, I consistently found the charismatics to be more effective and powerful speakers. Take, for example, these typical reactions from the subordinates of charismatic leaders:

> I enjoy listening to him—it can be very exciting at times. I wish I were ten years younger. He's so visionary when he speaks—as he says, the whole structure of financial services has to change in a model way unlike any we've known. He presents a tremendous challenge.

> He fills the room with ideas, challenges . . . hell of a job stimulating, exciting, you and the group. He's very engaging. He puts the force of his personality behind his ideas, and he gets you moving toward an idea as quickly as he can. You know he's found something important. He engages by building to a crescendo.

> He has so much enthusiasm that it spills over [in his talks]. He was always enthused, always high, but now it's right off the scale.

From these descriptions we see how charismatic leaders present their ideas in truly visionary ways, create engaging dialogues with their audiences, structure their talks like symphonies, and use their personal energy to radiate excitement about their plans. Now contrast these responses with comments from subordinates of several noncharismatic leaders:

> He can often be very detailed in his speeches covering a lot of ground. . . . He generally reads them from a prepared manuscript so there's not a lot of dynamism. I think it's because he doesn't want to make a mistake. He really leans towards being a perfectionist.

> He speaks in a very businesslike tone. It's really a monotone. I'd say he's not an exciting speaker. But his topics are informative. For example, he'll explain current capital budgeting plans or sales trends in different markets or the company's general strategy.

> Most of his speeches are pretty dry. He'll talk about the company's financial position or our strategy. It's usually quite concrete, not much in the way of abstractions. He comes across as a nice down-to-earth person. He's not charismatic like John F. Kennedy or another politician.

Speaking style, then, appears to have a significantly different impact if we compare the two types of leaders. There is a remarkable difference between the two sets of perceptions—clearly the noncharismatics are seen as less inspiring. But why is speaking so important to charisma?

The Importance of Language

If we think of leadership as essentially a process of influencing others, then language becomes one of the key means of social influence: "Sharing a language with other persons provides the subtlest and most powerful of all tools for controlling the behavior of other persons to one's advantage" (Morris, 1949, p. 214). Some have gone so far as to say that leadership is simply a "game of language" (Pondy, 1978). Thus we might reassess the effectiveness of leaders in terms of their ability to make the organization's work *meaningful* for employees. The task of leadership then becomes a matter of infusing day-to-day work with a larger sense of purpose and intrinsic appeal. To accomplish this, the leader must not only be able to sense meaningful opportunities in the environment but also to describe them in ways that maximize their significance. Martin Luther King, Jr., not only had a dream for black Americans, for example, but he could describe it in ways that had deep meaning. As we saw in the previous chapter, Steven Jobs performed a similar role as he described the mission of the Next computer company in terms meaningful for his organization. The charismatic leader, then, not only has the capacity to recognize important opportunities in the environment at large but also the ability to put them into descriptions that are full of significance for organizational members.

In this process of making work meaningful, leaders must also be skillful persuaders. While a leader can attempt to mandate by edict or coercion, the emotional energy of freely chosen commitment by subordinates is more powerful. As well, executives in large bureaucratic corporations may not possess the power to dictate organizational activities. Instead power may be so distributed that an executive is unable to mandate the implementation of specific goals. The ability to persuade then becomes a more critical skill. David Lamb (1987, p. 9) concludes from a study of eighty-nine CEOs: "In the long run, managers will not follow a strategy they do not believe in . . . a CEO is very much a politician. He must persuade others of the merits of his strategy . . . the CEO must sell himself, his organization, and his plan clearly." This process of building commitment to goals involves persuasion more than anything else. And persuasion depends upon highly effective language skills and ultimately an appeal to the emotions. More so than noncharismatics, charismatic leaders attempt to engage subordinates at this level. Intuitively or not, they seem to sense that the heart and soul are far greater energizers than the mind and logic.

Compare, for example, Steven Jobs's opening comments to his staff in Chapter Three with those of a noncharismatic leader I studied (Conger, 1985). This executive, like Jobs, is describing his organization's mission for the next year:

> Good morning, and welcome to our sixth Annual Management Meeting. As in the past, the purpose of the meeting is to review and discuss the overall objectives for 1986. . . . I am certain 1986 will be another successful year. The goals are high and consistent with prior years' objectives. As in the

past, our principal objective will be to accomplish our case [beer] sales goal while limiting price-off promotional activity. Control of operating expenses—throughout the company—will be the key to successfully reaching our profitability goals— especially in view of the economic environment in which we are presently operating. Last week we presented the operating and capital budgets to the Corporate Staff for approval. I am pleased to report that the budgets were generally approved and the Corporation has made available up to $39 million of capital to support the growth and improve the profitability of the Beverage Division. This is an increase of approximately $7 million over last year's capital budget of $32 million and is, indeed, an expression of confidence in the ability of the management of this division to cultivate and exploit the potential of our various markets.

We have an obligation to prudently employ this capital to those areas of the business where it will be most productive and profitable for both the short term and more importantly the long term. Incremental and profitable case sales are expected where developmental capital is invested. Each manager will be responsible for generating a 20% return on all developmental capital invested.

He continues with further descriptions of budgeting and human resource issues. What we see here is a straightforward exposition of the company's operating goals, budgets, and policies—devoid of any visionary and emotionally appealing purpose and focused instead on static operating details. The language is relatively mechanical, too, and there is no emotional content—in sharp contrast to Jobs's expressive and visionary discourse.

The Uses of Rhetoric

In the previous chapter we focused on the content of the leader's vision. Now our attention is turned to the process by which the vision is communicated. For while the charismatic's message is important, the process by which it is communicated appears to be even more significant. As political scientist Ann Ruth Willner (1984, p. 152) observes: "The major messages of charismatic political leaders have generally been propounded by others . . . and it is not uncommon for two speakers to present the same points of view on the same subject to the same audience and receive different responses. . . . Rhetorical spellbinding and the charismatic effect are produced less by logic and ideas than by emotional stimuli . . . in short, by the style of verbal communications." The leader's words exert their greatest impact as symbols rather than as literal meanings.

This point is well illustrated in political history. In Russia during the overthrow of the czar, for example, a Marxist movement was already in existence before the appearance of the charismatic Lenin. Two leaders of this movement, Plekhanov and Martov, advocated the same message as Lenin's, yet neither would develop Lenin's charismatic appeal. An energizing and hypnotic speaking style set Lenin apart, for "no one could so fire others with their plans" nor did anyone else possess "the secret radiating from Lenin of [a] positively hypnotic effect" (Tucker, 1970, pp. 79–80). Along with greater passion, Lenin had the greater gift for language. Apart from their appeal to emotions and ideals, charismatic leaders use a number of rhetorical techniques such as metaphors and analogy or different language styles or rhythmic devices to ensure that their message has a profound impact on their audience.

Metaphors, Analogies, and Organizational Stories. Metaphors and analogies draw a relationship of likeness between two things—often very unlike things—and are used for vividness, for clarification, or to express certain emotions. By a figurative comparison with a pool of water, for example, John F. Kennedy conveyed the need for politicians to temper themselves through more intellectual influences: "The political profession needs to have its temperature lowered in the cooling waters of the scholastic pool." They can also serve as interpretations or illustrations of reality—to teach complex issues, for instance. Metaphor and analogy capture an experience by appealing simultaneously to the various senses of the listener. As we will see, there is an appeal to the emotions, to the intellect, to imagination, and to values. This variety of stimulation ensures a more vivid experience for the listener.

Lee Iacocca has been particularly adept in the use of metaphor and analogy. In explaining a decision to cut his salary to one dollar, for example, he invoked the war metaphor of a commander joining his troops in the trenches (Iacocca and Novak, 1984, p. 230): "I didn't take one dollar a year to be a martyr. I took it because I had to go into the pits." He then draws an analogy to the family: "I call this equality of sacrifice. . . . It wasn't the loans that saved us, although we needed them badly. It was the hundreds of millions of dollars given up by everybody involved. It was like a family getting together and saying 'we've got a loan from our rich uncle and now we're going to prove that we can pay him back.' " By invoking this analogy of himself and Chrysler as a family, Iacocca attempts to create a strong identification between himself and the average Chrysler worker. As well, he interprets the hardships that Chrysler employees must experience as necessary to help the "family." This is a skillful rhetorical tactic because it plays on emotions associating the Chrysler situation with traditional family values. By tying the company crisis to a positive analogy, workers are provided with a rationale for their difficulties and the motivation to prove their worth as a family to Uncle Sam (Westley and Mintzberg, 1988).

Mary Kay Ash is another business leader who commonly employs metaphors in her talks. One of her more popular metaphors is the bumblebee, which she uses to describe the reality of the women who work for her. "You see," she explains, "a bee shouldn't be able to fly; its body is too heavy for its wings. But the bumblebee doesn't know this and it flies very well." Mary Kay explains the message of this metaphor: "[Women] come to us not knowing they can fly. Finally, with help and encouragement, they find their wings—and then they fly very well indeed" (Tunley, 1978, p. 5).

If we put ourselves in the listener's position, probably we will visualize an oversized bee that is flying with grace and speed. The listener then goes through a mental process of deciphering what the message means on a visual, cognitive, and emotional level. There is often a moment of puzzlement trying to decode the message; this pause ensures that the listener is both stimulated and concentrating on the speaker's message. In this case, the metaphor presents a paradox—something that should not fly but does. It is also a paradox that ends on a positive note— the creature is able to fly. Listeners then interpret this paradox in terms of themselves.

For Mary Kay's audience, the bumblebee metaphor captures the dilemma of the North American housewives to whom Mary Kay is appealing. These women have been child-bound and house-bound with little sense of their ability to build a successful career and develop financial independence. They have not seen their own wings. The metaphor provides an image of freedom through the notion of flying. By joining the Mary Kay organization, the metaphor is saying, women can achieve a sense of freedom through their own cosmetics business.

The metaphor also suggests that it is others' expectations that have kept housewives unaware of their ability to fly. There is an implicit reference here to society and men. Mary Kay is essentially saying: "You can fly. If others have said you are not constructed for success, it is only because they do not know the true powers hidden within you." The message brings the locus of control back to the person. "You already have this ability within you. You do not need to search for it. It is already yours." In this case, a simple metaphor is able to convey a powerful and uplifting set of messages.

Why are metaphors and analogies so powerful in communicating ideas and goals? And are they more powerful than arguments supported by logic and statistics? I ask these questions because the vast majority of business people do not use rhetoric in their communications. Instead corporations and MBA programs encourage careful, planned analysis presented with a wealth of supporting statistical information. The presenter delivers his or her message often in a monotone without emotion. While a logical delivery style is critical to effective decision making, this style has become so ingrained that managers use a similar format in speeches, in pep talks to their organizations, and in discussions with customers and analysts. Charismatic leaders, on the other hand, more often use such forums to "orate" and to convey their messages through metaphors, analogies, and stories.

Two streams of research support the greater impact of metaphors and analogies over rational discourse. The first comes from the field of speech communications. According to Osborn and Ehninger (1962), both of these rhetorical devices appear to excite the listener's imagination and create consecutive states of tension (puzzlement and recoil) and then release (insight and resolution). As noted earlier, listeners are engaged by the metaphor or analogy. They are not passive receivers of information but are triggered into a state of active thinking as they puzzle over the meaning of the story and attempt to make sense of it. After a period of puzzlement, they decipher its meaning and experience a sense of insight. They make sense of the story to explain their own situation. This process is so engaging that it commands the listener's attention and interest. Indeed, metaphors can even trigger an attitude change among listeners (Bowers and Osborn, 1966).

Studies from social psychology explain why these rhetorical devices are such persuasive and effective means of communicating ideas. It has been found that people treat statistical summaries as if they were uninformative (Borgida and Nisbett, 1977). This type of information appears to lack impact because it is abstract and colorless. In contrast, brief, face-to-face comments have a substantial impact on decision making. One might conclude, then, that information is used in proportion to its "vividness." By providing more vivid information and using concrete language, speakers can have a greater impact on their audience.

Experimental studies have been conducted recently to determine if stories are a more effective means of creating commitment than other forms of information such as abstract policy statements or statistical data (see Martin and Powers, 1983). Stories, for example, appear to convey more vividly values and behavior that are important to an organization. One story I often heard repeated in company interviews reinforced the necessity of being able to cope with the unexpected. The story went like this: An MBA candidate was being recruited by the firm. At the end of a day of interviews, he had met with everyone except the company's charismatic president. Up until this point, there was a clear consensus that the young man should be hired. At 5:30 P.M. he met with the president, who promptly asked if he would join him with another manager for drinks. Off they went to a nearby bar—at which point the president called his wife and the wife of the manager to join them for dinner. So the MBA proceeded off to dinner having yet to begin his interview with the president. Dinner ended at midnight . . . and still no interview had been conducted. The president then asked the recruit to come home with him for the actual interview. The young man balked with surprise, saying he was tired and needed to return home. He was not offered the position. The company president often repeated this story to illustrate that the qualifications needed by the company included a willingness to "roll with the punches" and "go the extra mile." The story was a far more powerful means of conveying these values than a directive from the president.

To test whether stories are in fact more effective than statistical information, a study was conducted to assess the effectiveness of an ad for a winery (Martin and Powers, 1983). The advertisement's aim was to convey the impression that the winery used the same winemaking techniques as those employed in the famed Chablis region of France. Along with an abstract policy statement, subjects randomly received this information in one of three forms: a story, a table of statistics, or a combination of the story plus statistics. The story included descriptions as follows:

> Joseph Beaumont's father spent most of his life growing grapes in Chablis, the famous winemaking area of France. . . . Before his father died, Joe promised him that someday he would make a California wine using the traditional winemaking techniques of Chablis. For ten years, Joe worked at some of the most famous vineyards in the Napa Valley, putting all his savings into a winery and

> vineyard, which he named Beaumont. . . . He or-
> dered special Limousin oak barrels, from the same
> suppliers used by Chablis winemakers. He filtered
> his wine using natural methods—egg whites rather
> than the chemical filters favored by other Califor-
> nia wineries. As Joe tasted his first vintage wine he
> thought, "My father would have been proud of this
> wine."

If participants received only statistics, a table was provided comparing the winemaking procedures (such as grade and barrel types) used at the winery, at other California wineries, and in Chablis. The study's conclusion was that those receiving only the story were significantly more likely to believe that Beaumont actually used the French procedures than the other two conditions. The story had a stronger impact.

From these and other results it appears that stories encourage commitment—in fact, greater commitment than other means of communicating information such as statistics. Their conclusions argue that the most effective tactic for managers is to communicate information about policies or their philosophy of management through an organizational story rather than through abstract information such as statistics.

It also appears that stories or metaphors are most potent when they invoke symbols that have deep cultural roots and, as a result, elicit strong emotions. In studies of charismatic political leaders, it was discovered that "the leader who becomes charismatic is the one who can inadvertently or deliberately tap the reservoir of relevant myths in his culture and who knows how to draw upon those myths that are linked to sacred figures, to its historical and legendary heroes, and to its historical and legendary ordeals and triumphs" (Willner, 1984, p. 62).

A magazine article recounting a speech by Steven Jobs to the Boston Computer Society in 1984 captures this use of historical myth and metaphor to evoke an audience's emotional associations with certain cultural symbols. It begins with a description of Jobs approaching the speaker's podium carrying with him a small beige case. The audience is aware that within the case is the company's new Macintosh personal computer, Apple Computer's $15 million response to IBM's recent entry into the home computer market:

> Taking an aggressive stance behind the podium, Jobs smiles, his face suddenly illuminated on the giant rear-projection screen mounted behind him. For anyone familiar with the Macintosh sci-fi commercial—a takeoff on George Orwell's *1984* . . . there is an immediate and delicious irony: instead of Big Brother's (read Big Blue's [IBM]) intimidating visage staring down from the wall, here is Steve Jobs'. He begins to speak.
>
> "The year is 1958, and a small company has succeeded in perfecting a new technology. It is called xerography. IBM has the opportunity to acquire rights to the new technology but elects not to. Thus, Xerox is born."
>
> Jobs reads on like a hyped-up Edward R. Murrow delivering a condensed history of post-chip technology: 1968—Digital Equipment Corp. introduces the first viable minicomputer, and IBM dismisses the market; 1978—Apple jumps into the home-computer field, IBM ignores it; 1981—IBM finally brings out its own personal computer (hisses from the bleachers) and quickly dominates the trade news. Building to his main thrust—that Macintosh represents a new wave of home hardware— Jobs can't resist overreaching. His company, he posits, is "the last force for freedom" in the marketplace. The implicit threat: Fight IBM to the last bare desktop or surrender to the forces of evil. [Kahn, 1984, p. 83]

Through his story and allusion to "freedom" and "Big Brother," Jobs calls upon several important cultural myths and symbols. For one, he invokes the story of David and Goliath— the underdog forces of good that must fight and triumph against the giant forces of evil. The listener, at some level, makes emotional associations—feelings of positive regard for Apple, its difficult task, its courage. Negative feelings are aroused toward the giant IBM that attempts to crush this positive force. The references to George Orwell whose book *1984* enjoyed wide popular appeal among Jobs's generation also trigger audience associations with a menacing giant (IBM) or "Big Brother" who is seeking omnipresent control. It is the classic struggle between the forces of good (Apple) and evil (IBM). The word *freedom*, it is assumed, invokes historical associations with the American revolution—again, the theme of the underdog triumphing over tyrannical forces. Through these evocative stories and myths, Jobs is able to build within his audience a set of favorable emotions toward Apple and negative associations with IBM.

As well, Jobs uses a standard rhetorical device of identifying a single common enemy. Hitler himself noted the significance of such a tactic:

> As a whole, and at all times, the efficiency of the truly national leader consists primarily in preventing the division of the attention of a people, and always concentrating it on a single enemy. The more uniformly the fighting will of a people is put into action, the greater will be the magnetic force of the movement and the more powerful the impetus of the blow. . . . A number of essentially different enemies must always be regarded as one in such a way that in the opinion of the mass of one's own adherents the war is being waged against one enemy alone. This strengthens the belief in one's own cause and increases one's bitterness against the attacker. [Burke, 1973, p. 193]

Gearing Language to Different Audiences. In addition to the use of metaphors, the level of the language, whether elevated or colloquial, is important. My own research suggests that charismatic leaders may be more adept at tailoring the level of their language to different audiences than other leaders. A colleague of one executive I studied described this ability: "He could just tune in with any group; he could charm senior people and could be at home with a new college graduate. . . . His message depends on the audience. He has a clever way about this. He has an excellent speech writer. He would say, 'Here's how I would like the message.' When the talk was completed, it always contained the right message for that audience. He and his speech writer could tune in on any audience." This was a typical description I heard when researching charismatic leaders. *Inc.* magazine, commenting on Donald Burr of People Express, remarked: "He moves effortlessly from the blunt, almost slang, of a working-class neighborhood to the polished diction of the corporate boardroom" (Rhodes, p. 45, 1984).

It would appear, however, that the ability to speak colloquially is particularly conducive to creating charismatic appeal. Franklin D. Roosevelt consistently used colloquial language and folk imagery to convey his ties to the person on the street. In fireside chats, for example, he would use sports analogies: "I have no expectation of making a hit every time I come to bat." Popular during his time were figurines and representations of three little monkeys who saw no evil (eyes covered), spoke no evil (mouth covered), and heard no evil (ears covered). In a campaign speech in New York City, Roosevelt would evoke their image: "For twelve years our Nation was afflicted with hear-nothing, see-nothing, do-nothing government" (Willner, 1984, p. 159). He consistently tailored his public talks to the man in the street. But why might this be such an effective technique?

A high-status figure such as an executive is expected to use an elevated style of language. When unexpectedly the every-day language of a plant worker is used, it may create a special positive response. A sense of equality with someone so elevated may at times produce a sense of affection and admiration. This element of the ordinary in someone so significant makes the latter seem even greater (Willner, 1984). This is certainly a practice commonly employed by Chrysler chairman Lee Iacocca, whose blunt and crisp language is reminiscent at times of a production supervisor. In another case, one senior manager described the charisma of his boss to me: "He would go into the plants and tour them, talk to the employees—'tell me what you're doing today.' . . . He'd skip levels downward just to get a comfort feeling, a name, a face. People really felt comfortable with him. They felt he understood them. He could relate and speak at their level. That was an important part of what attracted people to him." This is a consistent description of the charismatic leaders I have studied. Not only do they use the language of the everyday person, but they illustrate their ties to the common person through stories. Mary Kay, for example, is well known for her public comment: "Every night on my drive home from the office I forget that I'm chairman of the board, and remember that I'm Mel's wife" (Tunley, 1978, p. 5).

Speech Techniques. Another component of rhetoric is related to sound: repetition, rhythm, balance, alliteration. While such techniques have been largely restricted to religious and political leaders, the possibility of their use by business leaders should not be overlooked. A certain rhythm can often mesmerize an audience. In a study of charismatic political leaders, it was noted: "One need not even have understood German or Indonesian to have appreciated the force and quasi-hypnotic power of the crescendo effects built up by Hitler's and Sukarno's remorseless repetitions of key phrases in progressively louder tones" (Willner, 1984, p. 153). In his speeches Roosevelt often employed alliteration—the repetition of initial consonant sounds in two or more neighboring words or syllables. In describing the leadership of the Depression, he states:

> Those who tilled the soil no longer reaped the rewards which were their right. The small measure of their gains was decreed by men in distant cities. . . . Individual initiative was crushed in the cogs of a great machine.

The message was heightened by alliteration of the following letters: *r, r, r, d, d, i, i, c, c* (Willner, 1984, p. 164). This device creates an attention-holding rhythm.

Martin Luther King was a master of repetition and rhythm. This excerpt from his famous "I Have a Dream Speech" captures his abilities:

This will be the day when all of God's children will be able to sing with new meaning—"my country 'tis of thee, sweet land of liberty, of thee I sing; land where my fathers died, land of the pilgrim's pride; from every mountain side, let freedom ring"—and if America is to be a great nation, this must become true. So let freedom ring from the prodigious hilltops of New Hampshire. Let freedom ring from the mighty mountains of New York. Let freedom ring from the snow-capped Rockies of Colorado. Let freedom ring from the curvaceous slopes of California. But not only that. Let freedom ring from Stone Mountain of Georgia. Let freedom ring from Lookout Mountain of Tennessee. Let freedom ring from every hill and molehill of Mississippi, from every mountainside, let freedom ring. And when we allow freedom to ring, when we let it ring from every village and every hamlet, from every state and every city, we will be able to speed up that day when all of God's children—black men and white men, Jews and Gentiles, Protestants and Catholics—will be able to join hands and to sing in the words of the old Negro spiritual: "Free at last, free at last; thank God Almighty, we are free at last."

King first introduces rhyme and rhythm through the phrase "let freedom ring" and through excerpts from the song "America": "My country 'tis of *thee*; sweet land of liber*ty* . . ." This creates a rhythmic effect and stirs emotional associations with patriotism. King then moves into repetition of the key phrase "let freedom ring," over and over, at a progressively louder but still rhythmic tone, closing with repetition of a second phrase, "free at last." Repetition and rhythm, in this case, strike the listening audience in two important ways. First, King is able to create a songlike crescendo much like a combination of a symphony and Negro spiritual. This mesmerizes, captures attention, and builds emotional commitment to the message. Second and more important, he is able to leave his audience with one critical idea: They are to be free. Repetition ensures recall. Speech is more difficult to comprehend than the written word. Once spoken, the speaker's words are gone except for the listener's ability to remember them. If the speaker makes numerous points, the listener is not likely to recall them all. As well, the listener must be able to understand the speaker's ideas. The problem is that the listener has little time to pause for reflection. Repetition focuses the listener on the key ideas and drives them home.

Paralanguage, the *sound* of speech, is another key component of effective communication. Through appropriate paralanguage, one can communicate an image of self-confidence and power. When speakers are nervous and lacking in confidence, for example, they speak at a lower volume and make more numerous speech errors such as incomplete sentences, long pauses between words, and omitted portions of words or sentences (Kleinke, 1975; Schlenker, 1980). A confident speaker avoids these mistakes.

Recent research has also found differences between what are perceived as powerful and powerless styles of speech resulting from paralanguage and the use of certain words (Erickson, Lind, Johnson, and O'Barr, 1978). The powerless style includes speech hesitations such as "ah," "you know," and "uh"; polite phrases like "please" and "thank you"; questioning voice tones at the end of declarative statements; and such hedging phrases as "I think," "I guess," and "kind of." The powerful style lacks these qualities and instead portrays the speaker as more assuming, more goal-directed, more straightforward. A study of these two styles found that participants rated speakers using the powerful style as more potent, more attractive, and more credible (Erickson and others, 1978).

Finally, body movement to accompany speech appears to heighten the impact of language. Most of the charismatic leaders I have observed use body gestures extensively (especially their hands and facial expressions) to highlight and dramatize their ideas. Donald Burr's patterns of movement are described as those of an evangelist: "When friends or business associates talk about Donald Burr today, they invariably say, 'He could have been a preacher' . . . 'preacher' because it conveys exactly the right sense of sweating-in-a-hot-tent, evangelical fervor that makes the pulse race. Burr works hard when he talks. He paces; he sits; he stands; he throws out his arms" (Rhodes, 1984, p. 45). The noncharismatics, by contrast, tend to use less movement in general or at times indulge in nervous gestures such as shaking change in their pockets or more rigid body posture. Overall, they appear less animated.

The Notion of Framing

One of the most important concepts in rhetorical discourse is the notion of *framing*. Frames are symbolic structures that we use to make sense of our personal and social experiences—the perspective from which we interpret experience. And in a larger sense, they also provide a map for action. If we believe the world is flat, we will "frame" or interpret reality through that perspective and act accordingly. We are less likely to go sailing toward the horizons of the world than someone who believes the world to be round. In one study, participants were told of a project having an 80 percent chance of success or of a project having a 20 percent chance of failure and then asked to choose one for an investment. Inevitably they chose the former. Yet both descriptions are of the same outcome. By framing or wording an opportunity in a particular manner, we influence our perceptions of its outcomes quite profoundly.

The concept of frames is particularly important in rhetoric. In describing a mission or state of affairs, a leader is essentially framing it to interpret reality for followers. We have seen Steven Jobs framing the destiny of Apple Computer as a battle with the giant IBM and as a force in revolutionizing education. Jobs could have framed the mission purely as producing a better personal computer. Instead he casts the mission as a battle and a social contribution. If accepted, these interpretations become a shared perspective on reality. We must remember, though, that they may or may not interpret reality accurately. Indeed, the leader may distort reality in order to maximize commitment and motivation. He might construct a scenario of impending crisis, for example, simply to unfreeze and mobilize his organization. The leader's persuasive abilities then determine whether it will be believed or not. Some leaders are quite skillful with this tactic.

One organization that I studied was a regional telephone company undergoing separation from its parent organization, AT&T, during deregulation. The organization's members were feeling great anxiety over the accompanying loss of revenue and product support from their parent. There was much concern that the company would essentially fail to perform in the new deregulated environment. The senior executive at the time carefully reframed the organization's future from one of great uncertainty and turmoil to one of unusual and highly promising opportunity. He described the company as being on the cutting edge of new service and product opportunities and downplayed the uncertainty and danger. By describing this perspective on the future, the executive was able to restore a sense of assurance. A colleague said: "His vision is that in spite of all that has happened to the business, the future is a positive one. Take the best from what we were to innovate to be even better and unburden those things that could be cumbersome. The vision builds a sense of security. When the world seems to be falling down on us, he says we are a strong, viable company with opportunities we never had before."

This process has also been described as using "contexts of justification." In essence, the charismatic leader uses a structure of justifications to explain his vision, interpreting specific actions, events, and decisions in light of their meaning for the leader and the mission. Thus, for example, Lee Iacocca crafts a structure of justifications around his decision to lay off Chrysler employees. Drawing an analogy between the crisis at Chrysler and the crisis in America during World War II, he describes his role in closing the Chrysler plants through the metaphor of an army doctor on the front line: "I felt like any army surgeon. The toughest assignment in the world is for the doctor who's at the front during a battle. . . . It's a question of priorities. . . . They would pick the ones who had the best chance of survival" (Iacocca and Novak, 1984, p. 186). In drawing the link to an army doctor's role, Iacocca frames his intentions in a positive light. The plant closings were painful but done in the interests

of healing a wounded organization at war. He avoids more negative interpretations of his actions—the layoff of thousands of
workers (Westley and Mintzberg, 1988).

As well, by emphasizing confirming information or ignor-
ing contradictory information the leader can frame perceptions
of the viability of his or her vision. By providing volumes of
anecdotal information supporting a particular decision, the
charismatic leader may deepen his subordinates' confidence in
his judgment. In general, however, leaders have two means at
hand for framing interpretations of events, problems, or issues:
value amplification and belief amplification (Snow and others,
1986).

Value Amplification. If we think of values as ideas and behavior that are worthy of promotion and protection, then value
amplification is simply the process of elevating certain values as
basic to the overall mission. A skillful leader will select values
that have a strong appeal to subordinates and justify their activities in highly acceptable ways. If we return to Martin Luther
King's "I Have a Dream" speech, we can see clearly the importance of framing a mission around certain values. Though his
speech addressed the black man's plight in America, King purposely linked his mission to values that had great meaning for
white Americans. At the time of his speech, he had sensed a
growing positive shift among many whites toward his position.
As well, the Congress was considering President Kennedy's Civil
Rights Act of 1963. Sensing the possibility of support from society at large (and a nationwide television audience for his
speech), King choose to reach out to white America, framing
his struggle in values central to them. This decision contrasted
sharply from his earlier, more scolding approaches to white society. To make his appeal effective, King drew on lines from the
song "America"—lines that white Americans had sung as school
children—and quotes from Lincoln's Gettysburg Address and
the Declaration of Independence—lines Americans had recited
as school children: "I have a dream that one day this nation will
rise up and live out the true meaning of its creed: We hold these
truths to be self-evident, that all men are created equal." King's
inference was that if Americans truly believed in their country

and its values, then they must also believe in civil rights: "If America is to be a great nation, this must become true." By framing his movement's values in terms of the nation's values and their protection, King heightened the significance of the black man's struggle for every American. By carefully framing his mission in this way, he maximized its potential acceptance by mainstream Americans.

Social movements have made particularly effective use of value amplification. In the peace movement, for example, commonly idealized values associated with democracy and liberty and equality were often used. Activists claimed these values as their "constitutional right" to speak out on national security and nuclear armament. By framing their mission in terms of the country's democratic principles, they attempted to define their movement as serving the national public by revitalizing such values as the freedom of speech (Snow, Rochford, Worden, and Benford, 1986). It was a clever tactic to have their radical image accepted as a part of mainstream America.

Business leaders may use similar techniques in framing their own organization's mission. In this case, the analogy with a social movement is quite appropriate, for some charismatic business leaders transform their organization's missions into pseudosocial movements. Mary Kay, for example, ties equal rights for women to her cosmetics company's mission: "My objective was just to help women. It was not to make a tremendous amount of sales. I want women to earn money commensurate with men. I want them to be paid on the basis of what they have between their ears and their brains and not because they are male or female."

In his turnaround of Chrysler, Lee Iacocca framed the need for a government bailout as preserving basic American values of the free enterprise system, entrepreneurship, and protecting American jobs.

> We were asking [the government]: Would this country really be better off if Chrysler folded and the nation's unemployment rate went up another

half of one percent overnight? Would free enterprise really be saved if Chrysler failed and tens of
thousands of jobs were lost to the Japanese? Would
our free-market system really be more competitive
without the million-plus cars and trucks that
Chrysler builds and sells each year? . . . We explained [to the government] that we're really an
amalgam of little guys, we're an assembly company. We have eleven thousand suppliers and four
thousand dealers. Almost all of these people are
small businessmen—not fat cats. We need a helping
hand—not a handout. [Iacocca and Novak, 1984,
pp. 208 and 212]

This is an appeal to the basic American values of free enterprise
and entrepreneurship. Iacocca clearly reframes the perceptions
of Chrysler as a monolith automobile manufacturer to a collection of thousands of small businesses spread throughout America's heartland without whom the country's cherished values
and competitiveness would suffer (Westley and Mintzberg, 1988,
p. 192).

Belief Amplification. Belief amplification is the second
technique for framing an organization's mission. Values, on the
one hand, refer to the goals that the leader or organization
wishes to promote; beliefs are the ideas about which factors
support or impede actions taken to achieve those values. There
are four basic belief categories that are important to organizational leaders in framing their mission: the mission or task's importance, the need for it, stereotypes about antagonists of the
mission (both within the organization and externally), and the
ability of the organization to succeed (Snow and others, 1986,
p. 470).

As noted earlier, beliefs about the importance of the leader's mission are a primary focus for charismatic leaders. These
leaders are often effective at describing the current situation as
intolerable and then framing their future vision as the only viable,
and certainly the most attractive, pathway. A speech by the

charismatic president of one of the data processing consulting companies I studied illustrates how one leader communicated this belief:

> Today the world is moving very rapidly towards decentralized data processing. There is a shocking rate of change. It is critical for us to understand this because the IBM salesman may soon know more than we will. In 1981, 1.9% of the total personal computers sold were made by IBM, today 21%. The challenge is very obvious. We must rechart our direction. Do not be fooled by our success to date. Our techniques which once were avant garde are now accepted. . . . The traditional DP knowledge base has matured. Now this information is available in books. Others have copied us. We must rechart our direction. Our task now is to move into immature products like pc's [personal computers] and distributed computers. The market for knowledge in these areas is huge. . . . For example, I cannot emphasize enough the critical role that pc's are playing. In 1982, the Bank of America had 500 of them; by 1984, they had 5000. . . . You have a real challenge not to become obsolete in the next three years with the growth of pc's and the move to decentralized data processing. You individually need to get yourself immersed, consumed by that marketplace. . . . Your role is to keep our firm at the leading edge as we have done before. Because if we fail to innovate over the next three years, we will have a timebomb on our hands. . . . The way we will stay winners is by contributing to the body of knowledge. We must be consumed by the process of delivering quality ideas, advice, and results to our clients. Our strategy is and must be intellectual leadership in the management of computers.

We see this leader driving home to his staff perceptions of a rapidly changing world filled with serious competitive challenges. A picture of dire consequences is painted if the company does not continue to innovate and address emerging niche markets (personal computers and distributed computers). He powerfully conveys the seriousness of the firm's future mission.

The second dimension of beliefs concerns why the mission has arisen in the first place. Mary Kay's explanation that her company exists to help women homemakers is an example. Steven Jobs speaks about the need that Next will fulfill as he reflects on an earlier experience: "I felt it the first time when I visited a school . . . and they had a whole classroom full of Apple IIs and I spent a few hours there and I saw these 3rd and 4th graders growing up completely different than I grew up, because of this machine. . . . And here was this idea [the Apple computer] taken through all these stages resulting in a classroom full of kids growing up with some insights and fundamentally different experiences which I thought might be very beneficial to their lives, because of a germ of an idea a few years ago" (Nathan, 1986, p. 12). The need for the Next computer company, then, is based on the belief that computers play an integral and highly positive role in education.

Stereotyping the antagonists of a mission is another powerful way of creating commitment and cohesion. Often beliefs about antagonists provide models of what the charismatic leader's organization is not. Earlier we saw how Steven Jobs used analogies with Orwell's "Big Brother" to depict Apple's antagonist IBM. By implicit assumption, Apple embodies the opposite qualities of IBM. It must be a quick-to-market, entrepreneurial, free-thinking organization. Charismatic leaders in large organizations often portray the corporate staff or other operations as bureaucrats or "coyotes" laying roadblocks in the way of their mission—implying that they themselves are more effective and more concerned about market success.

Finally, beliefs about the efficacy of the organization are critically important. In essence, they build confidence in the entire mission. A leader may draw analogies, for instance, to earlier proven successes in order to confirm the likelihood of the current mission succeeding. So when Fred Smith, the chief executive of Federal Express, explained why his Zap Mail project (a facsimile service) would succeed despite early failures, he offered this justification: "When you're trying to do something that's never been done before, it's really sophistry to think you can project out in the future a set of numbers and have reality correspond to that. We started Zap Mail off under one set of circumstances and assumptions, and predictably those assumptions were all wrong. It was very similar to the situation in the express business. We started that off with a series of assumptions that were totally erroneous, and it was only when we threw all of those away and really started the television campaign that got to be very famous . . . that the thing really ramped up" (Nathan, 1986, p. 29).

Here Smith is drawing a direct link between the slumping Zap Mail project (which ultimately failed) and the company's core express business (which ultimately proved highly successful). Both started out with the wrong assumptions, he argues, yet express mail eventually succeeded. The problems with Zap Mail, he says, are part of the natural progression of an ultimately successful product. He even uses the word *predictably* to assure the listener that indeed this is a very predictable process. The key to success is simply television advertising—implicitly he is saying that this is all that is needed to ensure Zap Mail's success. So he portrays the reality of the Zap Mail project as hopeful and attainable.

From Vision to Charisma

In summary, we see that it is not simply the act of creating a vision but rather the way in which the vision is conveyed that is critical to generating charismatic appeal. For charismatic leaders are "meaning makers." They pick and choose from the rough materials of reality to construct pictures of great possibilities. Their persuasion then is of the subtlest kind, for they interpret reality to offer us images of the future that are irresistible. We may hardly notice that the charismatic leader is persuading us, so convincing are his descriptions. He does all of this through language. In his choice of words, values, and beliefs, the charismatic leader builds a new reality to ensure commitment and confidence in the mission. Rhetorical techniques—metaphors, stories, repetition and rhythm, and frames—all help to convey ideas in the most powerful ways. They ensure that the vision is well understood, that it is convincing, and that its ideas spark excitement. For if the leader can make a distinct dream seem like tomorrow's reality, we will follow.

But before we choose to follow, we must form a foundation of trust in the leader. And while his interpretations of reality may be convincing, we often need tangible evidence that this figure has the expertise to achieve the vision's realization. For his part, the leader must somehow demonstrate that he is credible and committed to his vision—he must actively build the trust of his organization. This is the next step in the leadership process. In Chapter Five, we will see how charismatic leaders actually do this.

Chapter 5

Building Impressions of Trustworthiness and Expertise

To be a charismatic leader, it is not enough simply to have an inspiring vision or great powers of persuasion. The charismatic leader must also be able to build trust in his or her abilities to transform the ideals of a vision into reality. Because the vision is usually lofty and involves great risks, the leader must be able to convince subordinates that he or she actually possesses the skills necessary to achieve their goals. The charismatic does this in two ways—by appearing to be an extraordinary individual and by demonstrating an extraordinary level of personal commitment to the vision. In both cases, the charismatic leader uses certain types of behavior to convey such impressions.

Much of the charismatic's power comes from others' perceptions that he or she is unique—a one-of-a-kind leader. This perception leads subordinates not only to be drawn to these figures but to trust them. They seem so extraordinarily gifted that followers believe that these leaders *must* know the answers, or at least the pathways, to the vision's accomplishment. Leaders can create this perception of extraordinariness through their prior successes, personal talents, and persuasive skills, through unconventional behavior, and through shared values. I recognize that, with the exception of unconventional behavior, these characteristics may not always be distinguishing attributes. Noncharismatic leaders may have equally exemplary records of success and expertise, for example. They may also share the widely held values of their subordinates. Thus some of these qualities are the building blocks of leadership in general. I suspect, however, that with further exploration we will find that it is often a matter of degree. In other words, charismatic leaders may more actively promote themselves and their ties to shared achievements and values than do noncharismatic leaders.

Building Trust Through Expertise

To appear extraordinary, one must have a record of extraordinary accomplishments or at least create the impression of such accomplishments. In the careers of many charismatic leaders we often find just such records. Both Lee Iacocca and John DeLorean were associated with highly successful cars, the Mustang and the Pontiac GTO. Arch McGill is reputed to have been the youngest vice-president at IBM. Bob Lipp, the charismatic president of Chemical Bank, was responsible for the major turnaround in the retail banking operations of his bank and was renowned as the company's financial wizard. In his first year as an IBM salesman, Ross Perot made so much money that a promotion would have resulted in a pay cut—he filled an entire year's sales quota three weeks into the year! Mary Kay Ash was crowned the sales queen of Stanley Home Products by the second year of her first sales job. In the case of the two data processing executives already discussed, both had held professorships at prestigious Ivy League schools, Harvard and MIT. They had also been responsible for significant contributions to their respective fields. Other charismatic leaders with whom I am familiar have had some remarkable achievement either in terms of major accomplishments or a meteoric rise in their profession.

Success is particularly important since it validates the leader's charisma and affirms his or her extraordinary abilities.

In the political arena, we see Franklin D. Roosevelt achieving a remarkable number of successes in his first hundred days in office. He would request from Congress an impressive volume of legislative acts—all of which would be passed. These included a civilian conservation corps, emergency relief funds for states and municipalities, reforms to banking and securities markets, a farmer's aid package, and measures to save home mortgages. All these successes would lead to public perceptions of an extraordinary leader. Many charismatics, then, have demonstrated a pattern of success. They appear to possess a fund of talent and ambition that contributes to the credibility of their claims. Again, while this may not always be a distinguishing characteristic, it is perhaps critical if perceptions of charisma are to emerge.

Failure, on the other hand, demonstrates flaws in the leader's abilities and strips away the aura of extraordinariness. Failure has its greatest impact in the early phases of a charismatic's rise to power. Later, at the peak of a charismatic's power, followers may have made such an emotional commitment to the leader that they will find ways to dismiss or deny any suggestion of failure. In one company, a charismatic leader had committed significant resources to a money-losing new technology. Despite continuing losses over a three-year period, the leader still retained his charismatic appeal. To outsiders and industry analysts, it was clear that his technological venture was ill-fated from the start—superior technologies were being developed by competitors. Yet the organization remained committed to the point of losing tens of millions of dollars. The leader simply attributed the losses to start-up costs and claimed that success was always close at hand right up to the very moment the project was terminated. His organization had made such a commitment of resources and emotion to the project—and to their leader—that it was difficult to see either one objectively.

In addition to a pattern of successes, certain personal qualities or behavior perceived as unusual may contribute to the charismatic aura. Describing John DeLorean, one university professor said: "He was one of the best students I had. I can't think of one better. The whole thing seemed to be effortless for him, to come naturally" (Levin, 1983, p. 21). A classmate remarked: "He was a genius. It was that simple. He used to say he had a photographic memory and you had to believe it." Consider, too, these common descriptions I have heard from subordinates of charismatics: "He is so bright and perceptive—he's able to see things far into the future" or "He's different from the rest of the world because of his conceptual and strategic abilities—he's simply brilliant." In the companies where I have studied these leaders, there are always stories of the charismatic's abilities. These comments from subordinates are representative:

> When we first came together, I was on a study team of the hotel and hospital industry. We were trying to understand strategically all their communication needs. He grasped what a whole set of needs they had. . . . For instance, how do we measure the service that we provide to a hospital? Before, we had considered it like any other nine-to-five business whereas in reality a hospital operates twenty-four hours a day. He understood the full range of implications of this fact. . . . He was also able to see that we had to pick up nontraditional areas of communication that we had not known about. In another example, two technological innovations came up. He knew we had to get them to market because they were going to be far-reaching, something others never saw.

> He is very charismatic. Two things stand out. One, it boils down to his knowledge of manufacturing. He knows what he's talking about. He just has tremendous depth in this area. For example, when he first arrived, he restructured our manufacturing processes. These changes made a remarkable difference. We were able to get product out the door like never before. . . . Second, he gives the impression

> that he's one step ahead. He talks from a strategic
> point of view. People will say, "I wish I had said
> that!"

Many of these leaders, then, do possess genuine talents. But in
some cases their success may cause perceptions of these talents
to become increasingly exaggerated, and soon they come to be
seen as extraordinary.

Foremost among the talents described by subordinates of
charismatic business executives is the leader's sense of strategic
insight. What may distinguish these charismatic leaders from
other leaders is the perception that they possess exceptional
strategic as well as functional expertise to the point of being described as wise. This perception is responsible for subordinates'
high level of trust in their leader's vision and his ability to make
it happen. Subordinates believe they are in the presence of a
person from whom they can learn and grow tremendously. In
the numerous interviews I have conducted, subordinates never
felt they knew as much as their charismatic leader or that they
possessed his unusual level of strategic insight.

Part of this strategic skill might be explained by a pre-
disposition to conceptual thinking. Combined with a wealth of
experience, this characteristic may contribute significantly to
strategic abilities. As well, the charismatic leaders I studied were,
relative to their contexts, indeed significantly wiser than subordinates in terms of overall experience. Either these leaders
created or selected organizations where they would appear wiser
or else they were recruited because the firm lacked executives
with the charismatic's knowledge. In one company I analyzed,
the charismatic leader had been hired from the outside to help
with serious growth problems in the firm's manufacturing operations. He came to the company after many years of successful
manufacturing experience at a competitor. He casually told me:
"I've seen an average dollar growth rate of 35 percent a year ever
since I began my professional career." When he joined the new
company where he was to become a charismatic leader, its sales
were at $1 billion. He had already managed an operation with

revenues several times this size. His expertise and experience were therefore significantly greater than anyone else's. This situation permitted him to tell subordinates: "Stick with me and I'll get you out of this mess. You're all competent people, and there isn't anything here that I haven't already seen before." In a relative sense, he *was* wiser.

Arch McGill spent some sixteen years at one of the nation's premier technology companies—IBM—where he was responsible for developing and implementing computer systems strategies. He then spent a number of years directing his own telecommunications consulting firm, gaining broad exposure to the industry. He came to AT&T with an impressive background not only in telecommunications and computers but also in marketing. Compared to his peers at AT&T, he had significantly more marketing experience and far greater exposure to the major strategic trends in the telecommunications market. Again, he was wise relative to his organization.

In the case of charismatic entrepreneurs, the leader's expertise may have led to the development of a unique product or service. Relative to the rest of their industry, these pioneers are indeed the experts. This was certainly the case with most of the charismatic entrepreneurs I have studied. The founder of one software company, for example, was described as the industry guru. He had developed a highly successful software package for business applications. He then established a consulting firm to market his software. It soon became the industry standard. "His program has become a norm of the industry. It's a cornerstone of the business . . . he is really the expert. When he walks out into the world, he is the foremost expert," explained an executive at the company. So a number of these figures, particularly the entrepreneurs, are truly experts in their fields.

It is this sense of strategic expertise that encourages subordinates to look to their charismatic leaders for direction and insight about the marketplace. The leader's wisdom creates a basis for *trust* and also *dependency.* I say dependency because subordinates often say they feel as if they are in a "learning mode" in the presence of their leader and willingly accept their dependence on him as a source of personal growth. So the leader's talents and achievements are key elements in the trust-building process.

Apart from genuine accomplishments, *impressions* of expertise can be created—by claiming credit for others' accomplishments and by simply conveying an aura of expertise. In other words, actual successes may not always be needed. In the first case, the leader may claim successes for which, in reality, he is only partly responsible. We find John DeLorean and, to some extent, Lee Iacocca claiming credit for the Pontiac GTO and Mustang, respectively, when records show that both products were the result of a number of individuals. Political leaders often exaggerate their accomplishments in an effort to build their own heroic stature. Ferdinand Marcos, the former head of the Philippines, consistently made exaggerated claims of his successes. Indeed, government publications during his presidency described Marcos as the most decorated Filipino soldier during World War II. Investigations would later reveal that this "guerrilla fighter" had no such record. His claims were a complete fiction. Charismatics, then, may exaggerate their claim to achievements simply to create an appearance of extraordinariness.

As well, the charismatic may act in certain ways that convey impressions of expertise. To demonstrate intellectual prowess, leaders who are not genuine intellectuals may grasp ideas and information from quick readings or through briefings with subordinates. If they have a good memory, they can then convey the impression of a powerful mind and breadth of knowledge. Franklin D. Roosevelt was described as possessing an inexhaustible curiosity. He had "a startling capacity to soak up notions and facts like a sponge, and to keep this material ready for constant use. He could overwhelm miners with a vast array of facts about the dismal coal situation; he could impress businessmen with a detailed description of the intricacies of their enterprises" (Burns, 1956, p. 155). Benito Mussolini, too, was known to possess a prodigious memory. The story is told of the day he greeted a parliamentary historian who presented him with a book. Mussolini hastily skimmed through it and stopped to read a page or two that captured his attention. Later that day, he used the same material in a speech delivered to the Italian Senate. Admiring comments were made concerning his amazing knowledge of a particular parliament in the past. It is therefore not so surprising that one biographer would write that Mussolini had an "exceptionally wide knowledge of science and philosophy" (Willner, 1984, p. 145). By picking up an array of facts and ideas, then, the charismatic may create an image of wisdom.

Self-confidence is another quality that conveys impressions of the leader's expertise. If the figure demonstrates an unquestioning belief in the goals he articulates, they will appear all the more believable and realistic. Expressions of confidence, for example, are critical to building trust in the feasibility of a leader's vision. Steven Jobs remarked: "There's just a ton of work to do [with the vision], and a lot of times when you have to walk a thousand miles and you take the first step, it looks like a long ways. And it really helps if someone is there saying we're one step closer. The goal definitely exists, it's not just a mirage out there. So in a thousand and one little and sometimes larger ways, the vision needs to be reiterated. I do that a lot" (Nathan, 1986, p. 8).

Fred Smith of Federal Express commented in the early launch phases of Zap Mail, his company's electronic delivery service: "It is no longer a matter of will Zap Mail be successful, it is a matter of when and to what extent. The Zap Mail project is the difference between Federal Express in the years to come being a temporary phenomenon and perhaps a relatively interesting phenomenon on the scene, to one which becomes one of the great commercial successes of all times" (Nathan, 1986, p. 29). There is no question here of Smith's confidence in the success of Zap Mail. By 1986, however, the project did fail and was terminated by Federal Express with the company taking a $190 million after-tax writeoff. After the board of directors voted to do away with Zap Mail, Smith at the company's annual meeting would simply say: "It was not in the best interest of our shareholders, employees, or customers to continue on the present course."

Hitler, to take a more extreme case, publicly demonstrated

tremendous self-confidence. He once told a group of party journalists that his political infallibility could be compared to the pope's spiritual infallibility. He was known to have shouted to one of his lieutenants: "I never make a mistake! Every one of my words is historic!" Emotionally, however, Hitler gyrated between megalomania and doubt and depression (Willner, 1984, p. 148).

Apart from personal abilities and impressions of expertise, charismatics also build trust in their actions by their unconventional tactics. Lee Iacocca used government-backed loans, money-back guarantees on Chrysler cars, union representation on the board of directors, and advertisements featuring himself. All of these ideas were effective—and unconventional—tactics for the automobile industry. Arch McGill would use confrontation to promote his ideas in a culture valuing consensus and gentlemanly conduct. To subordinates, such risky behavior was interpreted as a sign of his commitment to his ideas and to changing the culture of AT&T.

Charismatic leaders in mature organizations may also use unconventional behavior to break down traditional status barriers between senior managers and subordinates. Such action further emphasizes their links to the "common man" and may heighten a sense of shared values. Bob Lipp often visited the retail bank branches of his division—highly unusual behavior for senior managers who traditionally had little time for such activities. A consultant to Chemical Bank remarked: "Bob shirks the perks of power. When Chembank moved to Park Avenue, everyone had architects designing their offices and installing elegant, expensive furniture. Bob did not. He also drove around in a station wagon rather than a chauffeur-driven sedan. This informality and countercultural behavior led to immediate rapport with his branch staff." Arch McGill employed a similar approach at AT&T. He abolished the reserved parking spaces for senior managers of his operating unit. In a company where the memorandum was the traditional means of communication, McGill used the telephone or personal visits. Memos from him were rare and usually short and handwritten. McGill was therefore perceived as highly accessible in contrast to other corporate executives. In both cases, Lipp's and McGill's unconventional behavior demonstrated their commitment to the average worker or manager and to notions of the organization as a team working together.

When such unconventional approaches are successful, they serve two purposes for the charismatic leader. First, because such approaches challenge convention, their success appears even more significant. (On the other hand, the failure of an unconventional approach is more likely to be accepted since unconventionality implies greater risk.) Second, unconventional approaches draw attention to the leader and highlight his expertise. It is not surprising that the press is drawn to report on the activities of charismatic leaders.

To build trust further, charismatic leaders must appear to share certain basic values, attitudes, and aspirations with their followers and subordinates. As well, the leader must be like his followers in certain readily perceptible ways to build the sense of a common bond. Lee Iacocca's mannerisms convey a certain character that is almost the stereotype of the exemplary automobile executive. Cigar-smoking and blunt, Iacocca gives the impression of an action-oriented, take-charge manager. His beliefs about "America the Beautiful," a conservative role for government, and a concern for the workers match in many ways the audience to whom he is appealing. Steven Jobs looks the part of the California electronics entrepreneur. His casual dress in a "California style," his down-to-earth but articulate language, and his desire to help society fit well with his audience of young, Californian, computer people.

Much of this impression of solidarity may not be deliberate on the leaders' part; after all, their personal history is often rooted in the same community as their constituents. The point is that a leader could strengthen this impression by dressing, acting, and espousing values according to exemplary stereotypes of his followers. This is not to say that charismatic leaders are not also great challengers of the values held by subordinates; rather, there is a baseline of values they must appear to share. Housewives working for Mary Kay, for example, must sincerely believe that one of her highest values is to "transform women into the beautiful people they are." A leader may have a hard time deviating from this core of shared values, especially in the early stages of power.

Building Trust Through Commitment

Apart from appearing to be an extraordinary individual, the charismatic leader must also appear highly committed to the cause. Charismatics present themselves not as seeking so much personal gain but demonstrating a deep concern for the needs of their followers. This principle is especially true when charismatics make their commitment appear extraordinary by taking on great personal costs or risks to achieve their goals. Risks might include the possible loss of power, authority, or finances or the potential to be fired or demoted because of a controversial stand or failed venture. Donald Burr sold his car, his home, and two condominiums and drained his savings to raise $350,000 for his new undertaking, People Express.

John DeLorean was renowned for taking risks at General Motors. One measure of loyalty at GM involved conforming as a team player, for instance. In this case, a team player meant being invisible in terms of publicity, respecting a common dress code, and having only standard office decorations. DeLorean, however, was often the center of media publicity. He dressed in a continental style with wide ties and colored shirts. When promoted to headquarters, he requested brighter carpets, restaining of the paneling, and more modern furniture. It is said that the person in charge of office decor apologized but refused to make the changes: "We decorate the offices only every few years. And they are all done the same. It's the same way with the furniture. Maybe I can get you an extra table or lamp" (Martin and Siehl, 1983, pp. 57–58). DeLorean's unconventionality demonstrated his commitment to a freedom of individual expression despite the risks of reprimand or other penalties. Taking these highly visible risks, he demonstrated to subordinates his beliefs about what was important and what was not and showed that he was willing to take career risks for his beliefs. The simple fact that DeLorean continued to be promoted despite his unconventionality also increased perceptions of his ability and expertise— adding to his aura of charisma.

In a case like DeLorean's, where the leader behaves contrary to the status quo of the corporation, the image of commitment and heroism is often magnified. Since the corporation is traditionally seen as more powerful than the challenger, the mantle of heroism may be placed on the charismatic leader's shoulders if he succeeds. It is the classic story of David and Goliath. From time to time I have found charismatic leaders in large bureaucracies using challenges to the status quo as a means of building their heroic image. Certainly this was the case with DeLorean and Perot at General Motors and McGill at AT&T.

A leader can also demonstrate commitment in smaller though equally symbolic ways. Constant travel to operating units or the marketplace or putting in long work hours, for instance, can be interpreted as signs of the leader's personal investment. The excitement in a leader's voice when speaking about his or her goals can convey impressions of great commitment. The leader's involvement in projects that are symbolic of the organization's overall mission is another means. A charismatic leader in the data processing industry, for example, purchased a personal computer when they first appeared. Subordinates described this event as symbolic of their leader's commitment to keeping the company at the cutting edge of knowledge. Arch McGill, too, became involved early on in personal computers. A senior member of McGill's team commented on the impression it made: "We concluded that it was important that we understand the personal computer market and what it meant to our future. Arch bought one and called every CEO and consultant who was familiar with them. He literally sucked in every personal resource with great intensity until he thought he knew as much as there was to know. . . . It showed a 'hands on' willingness to get involved himself. . . . We knew from his involvement that this was an important technology and one that we'd each have to understand and build our strategy around." These signs of commitment, then, not only build trust in the leader but also direct subordinates' attention to what is important.

In summary, the charismatic leader's influence rests heavily upon the issue of trust. Because of the great effort required to meet the leader's visionary goals, much greater commitment is demanded from subordinates than would otherwise be the case. To gain such loyalty, the leader must earn it through prior successes and by demonstrating certain unique abilities. As well, manipulative leaders may falsely claim credit for achievements to heighten their image of success or may simply engage in actions that convey an impression of great expertise. In either case, they must show their own dedication to the cause through activities showing high personal commitment or risk. This is the ultimate demonstration of their dedication to the mission. But after trust has been built in the leader's abilities, there remains the crucial step of transforming his goals into concrete reality. This is the most difficult aspect of the charismatic's mission. He often needs enormous motivational energy and devotion from subordinates to turn his ideas into achievements. The leader's lofty goals may forever remain a dream if he does not know how to harness and direct the energies of his subordinates. The next chapter explores how the charismatic leader does this.

Chapter 6

Empowering Others to Achieve the Dream

One commonly hears of charismatic leaders tapping unheard of motivation among their subordinates. Through various
means they appear to be very skilled at unleashing and directing
human energy. This ability is a must for charismatic leaders because their goals are often so idealistic that achieving them depends on long and sustained effort. Motivational energy has to
be deep and persistent if the organization is to succeed. The
leader must continually make subordinates feel powerful and
capable in order to sustain their effort and willingness to persevere. Without this reinforcement, their energies will wane and
the leader's dream will never be realized. And while other business leaders may use empowerment practices, I suspect that the
charismatic leader does so to a greater degree and often more
skillfully. As well, in this stage the leader must model through
his behavior the skills and values needed to transform the vision
into reality. For in many ways subordinates look to their leader
for guidance. They believe in his vision and expect him to set
the standards by which it will be accomplished. The initial task,
however, must begin with generating motivational energy.

Tapping Motivational Energy

Charismatics rely largely on a psychological process called empowerment to stoke the fires of motivational energy. Through this process they are able to heighten followers' belief in their ability to achieve the leader's vision. Essentially this process depends on what is called self-efficacy (Bandura, 1986)—the belief that one has the power to bring about certain results. It might be a salesman's belief that he can achieve a specific sales goal, for example, or a manager's belief in her ability to turn around an ailing operation. Empowerment, then, is essentially a process of strengthening subordinates' convictions in their own self-efficacy. These beliefs are critical because they determine the extent to which people will initiate and persist in attempts to master difficult experiences.

Just as important, these beliefs affect whether subordinates will attempt to cope with a situation, for people often avoid situations that seem beyond their abilities. Suppose a group of employees is assigned the task of developing a revolutionary new computer. Without conviction that they can indeed accomplish this difficult task, they may stumble in self-doubt and never realize their goal. When their self-efficacy beliefs are strong, however, people act with assurance and involvement even in situations that would normally be intimidating (Bandura, 1986, p. 194). In the computer example, team members are more likely to persevere and search for solutions if they believe in their abilities. Expectations, then, are a critical ingredient in motivating in such circumstances. If somehow a leader can dramatically strengthen these expectations, subordinates can accomplish seemingly impossible tasks.

With strengthened convictions, not only can subordinates undertake difficult tasks but they may also persist at them, for efficacy expectations determine how much effort people will expend in the face of obstacles. The stronger the self-efficacy expectations, the more active the efforts (Bandura, 1986, p. 194). As well, a positive outcome is not always necessary. When people are empowered, their personal efficacy expectations are strengthened, not necessarily their expectations about the outcome of their efforts. Thus employees can develop a "can do" attitude regardless of their hopes for a positive outcome. Even in failing to obtain results, subordinates may continue to feel empowered as long as their efficacy beliefs are reinforced.

In essence, then, empowerment heightens a person's willingness to attempt difficult tasks and to make sustained efforts without necessarily a concern for positive outcomes. Tasks that would have been judged too difficult are now perceived as feasible. Empowerment is critical for charismatic leaders because it allows them to mobilize their organization in the face of monumental challenges. Even though high and sometimes unrealistic expectations may be set by the leader, they will be accepted.

How does the charismatic leader empower subordinates? Essentially there are four sources for developing efficacy expectations (Bandura, 1986): actual accomplishments, verbal persuasion, emotional arousal, and observation of others.

Power Through Accomplishments

As subordinates accomplish difficult or complex tasks, they have an opportunity to test their own efficacy. Initial success will make them feel capable and empowered. Adept charismatic leaders appear to structure goals and tasks so that subordinates experience these initial successes. Such accomplishments build confidence and in turn greater commitment to the mission. Instead of introducing a new organizational structure nationwide, for example, the leader might institute the change in a single region. Or the leader might initiate a project in a specific area or with a specific group of people because it is more likely to succeed there than anywhere else. By beginning on a small scale, the leader can ensure rapid completion and focus his resources on increasing the likelihood of success. Having discovered the key success factors in a pilot project, changes can be introduced on a broader scale and are more likely to have immediate and therefore confidence-building success. These early successes strongly reinforce subordinates' sense of power and efficacy: "In order for change to spread throughout an organization and become a permanent fixture, it appears that early successes are needed. . . . Experience with change suggests that a direct positive experience by managers with the change may be at least as powerful, if not more powerful, than quantitative measures of success. . . . When individuals, groups, and whole organizations feel more competent than they did before the change this increased sense of competence reinforces the new behavior and solidifies learning associated with change" (Beer, 1980, p. 64).

As well, leaders can structure tasks and rewards so that perceptions of accomplishment are heightened. When Bob Lipp assumed responsibility for the demoralized retail banking operations of Chemical Bank (see Chapter Two), he established a two-step process to empower his branch managers. First, he decentralized authority overnight in the system, allowing branch managers the opportunity to have more direct control over their performance and accomplishments. As *American Banker* magazine explained:

> The secret of Mr. Lipp's success lies in the way he organizes the more than 260 unit branches, which handle individuals and small business. The manager of a Chemical branch is encouraged to feel like the president of a community bank. And the best of them truly radiate that spirit. Consider Dominick Principato, head of a Chemical branch in Lynbrook, Long Island. Mr. Principato is in the habit of calling his branch "my little candy store." In order to develop business for his candy store, Mr. Principato spends at least 25% of his time pounding the pavement, soliciting deposits from affluent individuals and knocking on the doors of mom-and-pop establishments in his area.

Each month, Lipp's office also published a master list showing results by office, by district, and by division. "They can see at the end of each month how they were doing," Lipp commented. This set the stage for interbranch competition. "Each month I'd call the top ten branches and congratulate them and say 'Take your staff out to dinner on me,' " remarked Lipp. (A "bottom ten" were also listed.) An overall bonus system was established: "The top twenty-five branches got a 'pot' they could split all the way down to the tellers." Managers, individually, could receive substantial rewards. Since Lipp's goal was to create a new attitude of "selling" among his managers, he changed the reporting system to one based on volume of business deposits rather than profit and loss. Lipp explained: "Many other banks rate their managers on the value of funds generated. But that's silly. The branch manager has no control over interest rates. What he can control is the physical volume of deposits, regardless of their transfer price. So when I took over the branches, I junked the previous measurement system, which made the branch manager a hero when rates rose but a bum when rates fell, and I substituted one based on volume." Branch managers could now immediately experience a sense of achievement based on their efforts and measure the outcome. "My philosophy of management," said Lipp, "is to measure people on a fair and equitable basis with *very clear and quantifiable goals*—not too many of them though." As well, managers received unambiguous signals from top management. They knew they would receive larger bonuses for bringing in more balances, regardless of whether these balances were worth 7 percent or 12 percent. Now they could be personally responsible for their achievements.

Lipp's measurement system and peer group competition were a dramatic change for the organization. One executive put it this way: "Lipp's idea was countercultural. The history of banking had been one of security for employees, not compensation or challenge. But competition and the industry were changing. When Bob came on board, the climate in the branches was very fuzzy. Bob brought clarity when it was needed. But a lot of people were afraid of his measurement system. The word was 'You have to produce—the B.S. is over.' There was dissatisfaction and fear from others in the bank that Lipp had his goals set too high, but with one-third of the branches registering dramatic increases, the soundness of his plan seemed to be confirmed."

As the branch managers began to meet their performance objectives, a greater sense of confidence and empowerment was experienced throughout the organization.

Within five years, Lipp was able to double retail and small
business deposits from $1 billion to $2 billion. He also turned
what had been losses in 1977 into an after-tax profit of $85 mil-
lion accounting for 40 percent of Chemical Bank's earnings in
that year. The key point is that Lipp created a system in which
his managers were in control of their own accomplishments. Because of his goals (deposit volume) and the measurement system's monthly results, managers could achieve almost immediate
performance feedback. As an outcome, they experienced tangible results of their success early on in the change process and
in turn were empowered to ensure the project's success.

In another case, a charismatic leader used a process he
called "seeding" to initiate performance accomplishments in the
early stages of a major reorganization. The setting was a highly
successful and rapidly growing computer firm; the leader was
the vice-president of manufacturing. He had been brought in
from the outside and was in the process of revamping manufacturing operations. Early on he found that the company's
costs on its terminal monitors were quite high. He had decided,
however, that he wanted his staff to discover the problem for
themselves and thereby find the solution. One day, he placed
behind his desk a black and white Sony TV with a placard on
top saying $69.95. Next to it he placed a stripped-down version
of the company's monitor with a placard saying $125.95. Both
placards reflected the actual costs of the two products. He did
not say a word to his staff. As department managers entered
their boss's office, they could not help but notice the two sets.
They quickly got the message that their monitor was costing
twice as much as a finished television set. Within a month, the
manufacturing team had redesigned the monitor and lowered its
costs by 40 percent. The boss had not said a word.

When I first heard of such an obvious message I wondered
why the boss was not more direct. Subordinates would be hard
pressed not to get the point. In fact, the boss appeared to be
hitting his subordinates over the head with the problem. Pre-

sented out of context this example hardly seems to make others feel more competent and powerful. Yet the staff described themselves as quite motivated by this behavior. Why, I wondered? A little later I found out.

Prior to the executive's arrival, the department had been managed by a dictatorial boss. He tightly controlled his staff's actions and stifled any sense of discretion. Implicitly his behavior said to subordinates: "You have no ideas of your own." He fired freely—leaving staff to feel they had little choice whether or not to accept his orders. By his actions, he essentially transformed his managers into powerless order-takers with little sense of their own ability. When the new vice-president arrived, he found a group of demoralized subordinates who were nonetheless quite talented. To restore initiative and performance, he began to demonstrate the seriousness of his intentions in clear and symbolic ways. Rather than telling his subordinates what to do as his predecessor had done, he started by seeding ideas and suggestions in humorous and indirect ways. The TV monitor is one of many examples. Only in this way, he felt, could he transform his staff from order-takers into performers while ensuring their sensitivity to critical problems. He also structured these experiences so that subordinates would have a measure of success: "From past experience, I knew what these guys were capable of. So in the beginning, I set them up in situations where I knew they'd be somehow able to accomplish the task. I wanted them to get some successes under their belts right away. As they succeeded, I raised the stakes a little bit higher each time." Gradually through these actions he was able to restore a sense of initiative and personal competence to his staff as they began to accomplish the seeded objectives. In essence, he created opportunities for his subordinates that restored their sense of initiative. This element of empowerment—creating genuine experiences of success—is by far the most potent of the leader's empowerment tools. It affirms subordinates' expectations about their abilities firsthand and as a result it strengthens these beliefs—leading them to regard the next difficult task as manageable. The danger, of course, is that a false sense of confidence may develop. At some point, their expectations could be-

come unrealistic and the truly impossible might be attempted—
ultimately leading to failure, crushed expectations, and wasted
resources.

Power Through Verbal Persuasion

When people are persuaded verbally that they have the
capacity to master a difficult task, they are likely to mobilize a
greater sustained effort than if they harbor self-doubts or focus
on their personal deficiencies when the going gets tough. Returning to Bob Lipp for a moment, we can see how one leader
effectively uses this particular technique.

After developing his strategy for the organization, Lipp
went on a personal tour of his 250 retail branches. His aim was
simply to express his confidence in employees' abilities to carry
out the new organizational goals. As he explained:

> I saw that the branch system was very down, mo-
> rale was low. They felt like they'd lost a lot of their
> power. There were serious problems and a lot of
> staff were just hiding. What I saw was that we really
> wanted to create a small community for each branch
> where customers would feel known. To do that, I
> needed to create an attitude change. I saw that the
> attitudes of the branch staff were a reflection of
> the branch manager. The approach then was a man-
> ageable job—now I had to focus on only 250 peo-
> ple, the branch managers, rather than the 3,000
> staff employees out there. I knew I had to change
> their mentality from being lost in a bureaucracy to
> feeling like the president of their own bank. I had
> to convince them they were special—that they had
> the power to transform the organization. . . . All I
> did was talk it up. I was up every night. In one
> morning, I hit seventeen branches. My goal was to
> sell a new attitude. To encourage people "to pump
> iron," I'd say "Hi, how's business?," encourage
> them. I'd arrange tours of the branches from the

chairman on down. I just spent a lot of time talking to these people—explaining that they were the
ones who could transform the organization.

It was a brilliant tactic—one that made the branch managers feel
special and important. It was also unusual. One executive told
me: "Bob would go out in the field to visit the operations,
which was very unusual for senior people in this industry." The
uniqueness of his visits helped to convince the branch managers
that they were special.

What Lipp did so skillfully was to recognize that his managers had the talent and energy to turn their operations around;
it was their sense of power that was missing. He recognized that
their pride had been hurt and that he needed to restore their
sense of self-importance. Through verbal persuasion and increased authority he had to convince them that they were no
longer pawns of the system—that they were indeed presidents of
their own banks.

As well, a leader can express confidence in subordinates
through highly visible and personal rewards. As we will see in
the next chapter, one of the most important rewards for the followers of charismatic leaders is the leader's personal approval.
Recognition from the leader, in essence, confirms one's self-
worth. It is also a sign that the subordinate belongs to a special
inner circle. For these reasons, recognition is highly sought after.
Charismatics seem to sense this dynamic and use it to empower.

The leaders I have studied took several approaches to personal rewards. To reward exceptional performance, one executive established the "I Make a Difference Club." Each year he
would select two or three staff members to be recognized for
their excellence on the job. It was a very exclusive club. Inductees were invited to dinner in New York City but were not
told beforehand that they were about to join the "I Make a Difference Club." They would arrive and meet with other staff
members for a "staff dinner." During dinner, everyone was asked
to speak about current events in their part of the company.
First the old-timers spoke. Then the inductees, still unaware of
their coming induction, were asked to speak. Only then were

they informed that they had just joined the club. The leader would close with words of praise for the new inductees. As one executive said: "It's one of the most wonderful moments in life." Essentially this club served as a means for the leader to express his confidence in star players.

This executive also made extensive use of personal letters thanking employees for their efforts on projects. A typical letter might say: "Fred, I would personally like to thank you for your contribution to . . . , and I want you to know that I appreciate it." Lunches and dinners were hosted for special achievements. Public recognition was used extensively as a means of rewarding, as well. One subordinate commented about his boss: "He will make sure that people know that so and so did an excellent job on something. He's superb on giving people credit. If the person has done an exceptional job on a task or project, he will be given the opportunity to present his or her findings all the way to the board. Six months later, you'll get a call from a friend and learn that he has dropped your name in a speech saying that you did well. It makes you want to do it again."

This practice of expressing confidence is especially empowering in large organizations. Some of the charismatics just mentioned were executives in enormous corporations that did little to develop a sense of an "I" held by employees—let alone an "I that made a difference." It was easy for organizational members to feel lost in the bureaucracy and for their achievements to be invisible. The leaders countered this tendency by institutionalizing a reward system that provided visibility and recognition—the "I Make A Difference Club," presentations to the board, names dropped in speeches. Suddenly you stood out. You were special.

In both the large and the entrepreneurial firms, outstanding performance was something of a necessity. All the executives had demanding goals to achieve. As such, they had to tend to their subordinates' sense of importance and contribution. They had to structure their persuasion and rewards to keep people motivated—to ensure that their confidence and commitment would not be eroded by the pressures placed on them.

But expressions of confidence and praise must be sincere

to be effective. As Jan Carlzon of SAS noted in his autobiography, to do otherwise essentially weakens attempts at empowerment: "Praise generates energy, but only if it is justified. Receiving unmerited accolades can be an insult that reveals indifference on the part of the bestower. At SAS, for example, we once 'thoughtfully' sent thank-you notes to all of the employees who had pitched in to alleviate the effects of a strike. But our effort was not administered carefully, so that even people who had nothing to do with the strike were congratulated. Our good intentions backfired as confusion and resentment ensued" (Carlzon, 1987, pp. 115–116).

Power Through Emotional Arousal

Another empowering practice used by charismatics is the element of play or drama. Its purpose is largely to stir up positive emotions. For example, every few months several of the leaders I studied would stage dramatic "up sessions" to keep the motivation and excitement of their staff going. They would host an afternoon or a one or two-day event devoted solely to building confidence. They opened the event with an uplifting speech about the future and then presented a special speaker who was inspirational. There would be films to build excitement or confidence—for example, a man making an ascent of a difficult mountain. The message was that this person was finding satisfaction in the work he does at an extraordinary level of competence. At these sessions, there would also be rewards for exceptional achievements. Mary Kay, for example, is famous for her annual sales convention where she awards top achievers with diamonds, cars, minks, and so on. Edwin Land would host extravaganzas at Polaroid's annual shareholder meetings to build excitement within and outside the organization. These ceremonial activities enhanced the personal status of company employees and revitalized the feelings of community that bound them together.

An element of play appears to be especially liberating in situations of great stress—an atmosphere commonly associated with the charismatic leader. It allows for the venting of frustration and also helps employees to regain a sense of control. Subordinates are able to step back from the pressure for a moment.

One charismatic leader, for example, was appointed the head of a troubled division. When he arrived, the unit was spilling over with problems. Demand had outstripped the division's ability to maintain adequate inventories, and product quality had slipped. His predecessors had been authoritarian managers, and junior managers were demoralized as well as anxious about keeping their jobs. As one told me, "You never knew who would be shot next." The leader felt he had to break the tension in a way that would allow his staff to regain their sense of power. He wanted to remove the stiffness and paranoia and turn an "impossible" task into something more fun and manageable.

So, I was told, at the end of his first staff meeting he quietly pulled out a squirt gun and blasted one of his managers with water. At first, there was a moment of stunned silence, then suddenly the room broke out in laughter. He remarked with a smile, "You gotta have fun in this business. It's not worth having your stomach in ulcers." Thus began a month of squirt gun fights between the leader and his managers.

The end result? A senior manager's comment is representative: "He wanted people to feel comfortable, to feel in control. He used waterguns to do that. It was a game. It took the stiffness out of the business. Allowed people to play in a safe environment. As the boss says, 'to have fun.' It restored rapport and morale. He also knew when to stop. We haven't used waterguns in nine months. It had served its purpose. . . . The waterfights were like being accepted into a club. Once it achieved its purpose, it would have been overdone."

Interview after interview with subordinates confirmed the effectiveness of this tactic. The event had been experienced as an empowering ritual. In most contexts, this behavior would have been abusive. Why did it work? The executive's staff was largely young males—"rough and ready" men who could best be described as fun-loving and playful. They were accustomed to an informal atmosphere and operated in a very down-to-earth style. The leader's predecessor, on the other hand, had been stiff and formal. The new leader's aim, therefore, was to quickly and powerfully convey his intentions of managing in a style distinct from his predecessor's. He was concerned, however, that his size—he is a tall, energetic, barrel-chested man—as well as his extensive background in manufacturing might intimidate his young staff and further discourage them from assuming initiative and control. Through the squirt gun fights, he was able to relieve tension and restore some sense of control, to emphasize the importance of having fun in an otherwise trying work environment, and to direct subordinates' concerns away from his skills and other intimidating qualities. This element of inducing play and positive emotions in the work atmosphere is used far too rarely in business today. Yet from this example and others I have seen, it seems to be an effective way of energizing or revitalizing an organization.

Power Through Vicarious Experience

The final technique that leaders can use to empower involves themselves. The leader is often the most visible symbol of the organization's mission. As well, subordinates come to believe that the leader knows what it takes to succeed so they may watch his or her actions closely. By demonstrating confidence in their own abilities and by undertaking some of the same tasks subordinates are expected to accomplish, leaders can model the outcomes of personal empowerment.

Returning to John DeLorean, we can see how he used countercultural behavior to defy elements of General Motors's culture that minimized individual autonomy and to exemplify self-expressive behavior for his subordinates. One of these actions involved the "airport ritual," a company rite that centered on deference to authority. This ritual reinforced the virtues of deference by requiring subordinates to meet their superiors from out of town at the airport. They would carry their bags, pay hotel and meal bills, and drive them around to engagements. On one occasion, DeLorean failed to meet his boss, Pete Estes, at the airport. Estes raged into DeLorean's motel room to find him in the shower. Estes yelled, "Why the hell wasn't someone out to meet me at the airport this morning? You knew I was coming, but nobody was there. Goddamnit, I served my time picking up my bosses at the airport. Now you guys are going to do this for me" (Wright, 1979, pp. 42–43). This incident illustrates the significance of the ritual—that helping superiors is a critical element of an executive's duties. DeLorean's failure to do so sent a clear message of disrespect for authority. Essentially his actions demonstrated that he was willing to assume the risks involved in defying company norms to say that such behavior was not in fact a priority for effective management. By undertaking these risky actions, he was modeling his own sense of power and confidence in the face of the GM hierarchy.

In a political environment like GM, DeLorean reinforced his countercultural values in other ways, too. He claimed, for example, he would always rely on objective criteria for appraising performance, even if the results ran counter to his subjective evaluation. He would support his claim by citing the story of a certain disagreeable individual whose performance record was superb. Despite his dislike of the person, DeLorean claimed that he had promoted him four times (Martin and Siehl, 1983, p. 61). In essence, these actions became models of behavior for DeLorean's subordinates. Because he succeeded in carrying out these tactics and in so doing affirmed his own values, his staff could experience vicariously their boss's heroic power. In turn, they could begin to gain self-confidence in their own ability to act similarly without fear of retribution.

Ross Perot, chairman of Electronic Data Systems, epitomizes this ability to exemplify self-confidence. In 1979, he arranged and participated in a mission to rescue two executives taken prisoner in Iran during the country's revolution. Perot's team was waiting to take the men overland to Turkey, when the Ayatollah Khomeini's followers opened the prison doors. While this is an extreme case of demonstrating empowerment, leaders can certainly create opportunities to model self-confidence and a sense of personal power.

In summary, then, empowerment is a critical element of charismatic leadership. It is in essence a generator switch for the leader in creating motivational energy. Interestingly, many of these techniques can be learned and used by managers and leaders alike. Once learned, they become a potent tool in maximizing an organization's human resources. But as these human energies are tapped, they must be clearly focused to be effective. Leaders must be actively involved in this process if they are to direct their enterprise to success. They must become both coach and teacher.

The Charismatic as Teacher

As the organization's motivational energy is developed, the charismatic leader must channel it into the attitudes, skills, and accomplishments that are necessary to realize his vision. Part of the charismatic leader's role, then, includes teaching and coaching. He becomes, as noted earlier, an impresario. Although all leaders—charismatic or not—serve in some capacity as "educators," charismatics have a more intense relationship with their subordinates than other leaders and, therefore, their teaching role is likely to be more intense. The charismatics I have studied have all carefully socialized and trained their subordinates. This applies to both charismatic entrepreneurs and those in management positions in corporations. In certain ways, however, the education process is more difficult for those in conventional firms since their subordinates are usually well socialized in traditional ways of doing things. These conventional mind-sets must be skillfully broken.

A wide range of formats and forums are used for teaching. In some cases, the leader will exemplify in his or her own behavior certain key values and skills. As the head of a consulting firm, one charismatic leader spent a significant portion of his time out of the office in the marketplace. He was in essence role-modeling for the firm an activity critical to the firm's success. A subordinate noted the lesson: "His chair is typically empty, he's off traveling. He's very oriented to the marketplace. He learns everything by talking to people out there. He's on the leading edge. It sets a value within our organization—'get out there and talk and listen to people.' He's molding a value." So the leader may not always be teaching in the traditional sense like a classroom teacher. Rather, modeling is sometimes the substitute for direct instruction.

In another case, the leader's actions continually drove

home the importance of being well prepared in one's work. At a conference, for example, a power shortage cut off lighting in the hotel's meeting room. The leader quickly went to his car and returned with a candle, matches, and a kerosene lamp. The meeting continued as if nothing had happened. "He was prepared for that emergency. We couldn't believe it. The moral was 'be prepared—anything can happen,' " remarked a manager at the conference. This leader's actions clearly demonstrated the values he believed to be important. He also valued perseverance and the ability to see beyond obstacles. One of the popular stories in his organization was a tale of how he was fogbound on an island with several members of his management team. Although flights had been canceled for the day and there appeared little hope of returning to the mainland, he had an important commitment later that day at his office. So instead of booking into a motel and waiting until the next morning to depart, he went to the dock, hired a whaling boat, got two cases of beer, and traveled home. Both incidents set clear norms of behavior for subordinates. The implicit message was obvious: "Here are the attitudes that help us achieve our goals—be prepared for any outcome and be persistent."

Another way of teaching involves setting subordinates up in experiences. As descriptions from the subordinates of charismatic leaders attest, this is a common practice:

> He's constantly creating situations for you to learn from. I wanted him to come to a seminar in New York. He said he could be there for only a few hours. The seminar was a day and a half. I'm sure he thought it would be better for me to do it myself. That I'd learn more. Having him there would have drawn the attention away from me. We never had any discussion of that but I'm sure he'd thought it out beforehand.

> He typically sets people up in experiences where they'll learn. For example, when he first arrived, he told me, "You've got to make 18,000 computer boards a month—that's your goal." Well, we had

been doing only 12,000 a month. But, you know, I actually succeeded! He was always there, though, subtly coaching me along. He knew he could push me. But he only pushes those he knows he can push. . . . Another time, he said to me, "Gee, you really need some international experience." Then it popped out again. So I knew I needed to set something up.

At other times, the charismatic leader might use experiences that disregard conventional expectations of behavior. This is a common tactic of charismatic leaders in mature organizations. A subordinate of one charismatic leader described how his boss fostered behavioral change: "You're making a presentation to him, and it will trigger something in his mind. He'll say, 'Call the president of General Motors.' He did a lot of that when he first arrived because he knew people here were very level conscious and didn't break the hierarchy. They weren't used to calling up executives. The presenter would say, 'I don't know what to say to the president of GM.' The boss's response was, 'Well, who can teach you all you need to know about this? Call him!' " Such experiences unlocked behavioral norms and permitted the charismatic leader to introduce cultural change.

More often these leaders use meetings or presentations by subordinates as a forum for teaching and socializing their values. Typically they challenge the basic assumptions behind a subordinate's presentation in such a way that the presenter begins to see the ramifications of his ideas or the role of the leader's values. Here is a representative comment about one of these experiences: "One of the greatest learning experiences you had was to make a presentation to [the charismatic leader]. He emphasized issue analysis—what were the real strategic issues, challenging you over and over, taking pieces of your presentation and blasting them out. He'd force you to understand the outcome you wanted to achieve in the broadest perspective. He'd challenge you to think it through. You'd grow right on the spot. He got us to do critical analysis and to present it in a far-reaching way."

Such leaders constantly force subordinates to see the

links between their task and the overall vision. A typical experience is captured by the quote of this manager: "We went through an industry profile of our group with [the charismatic leader] step by step. In all those interactions, he was constantly learning from us about our research and translating for us the relevance of our findings into market strategy. There was a lot of teaching and constructive criticism. You realized you were not doing the projects just to get data. . . . The value was that we were able to distinguish a discrete set of needs and in turn the provision of a discrete set of services. . . . He taught us that the concept of marketing was a corporate attitude, not just a function."

Finally, training sessions are commonly used to instill values and build specific skills. Attempting to build teamwork in a division characterized by self-serving individualism, one charismatic leader began his training sessions with a game called Mastermind. The game essentially teaches that a mutual "win/win" strategy for a player and his opponents is more effective than a "win/lose" strategy where no one gains. Since these sessions involved considerable interaction with senior managers, they promoted a sense of the organization as a team working together.

In conclusion, many charismatic leaders are skillful teachers and coaches. They are able to train their subordinates in new ways of behaving and into adopting new value systems. The ultimate aim of these changes is, of course, to provide the basic skills and values that the leader believes are necessary to achieve his vision. And in this process of teaching and building confidence, the charismatic leader initiates a bond between himself and his followers that is often unique among leaders. His abilities become the traits desired by subordinates. His approval becomes the ultimate source of confirmation. And as subordinates identify more and more with the charismatic leader, a mutual dependency develops. Ultimately it is the strength of this bond that creates the powerful qualities associated with charismatic leaders—their ability to motivate, for example. In the next chapter we will examine the outcomes of these ties that bind the leader and those being led.

Chapter 7

Encouraging Extraordinary Commitment in Followers

We have seen that charismatic leaders expend an enormous amount of energy on persuading, on motivating, and on instructing the members of their organizations. In comparison to other leaders, this attention to subordinates seems all-consuming. Remember, however, that the goals of the charismatic leader are set exceptionally high and that charismatics appear to derive their satisfaction more from artful persuasion than from direct commands. They may also sense that by creating perceptions of a freely chosen commitment they can tap deeper reservoirs of motivational energy within their subordinates. But it would be misleading to say that the power of charismatic leaders resides largely in their persuasive abilities. In reality, the various stages of the leadership process are laying the groundwork for a powerful bond that is unique to charismatic leaders. It results in performance that is often far beyond expectations and certainly beyond that achieved by most organizations. It also results in a level of commitment and loyalty to the leader and his mission that is quite rare.

In this chapter we will take a look at how the stages of charismatic leadership (visioning, communication, trust building, and empowerment) work their cumulative effects on followers to create this bond of unusual intensity between the leader and the led. We will then see how this tie produces performance beyond expectations. We look first at the type of people who are attracted to charismatic leaders, for here, some argue, lies the secret to the extraordinary outcomes of charismatic leadership.

Profile of a Follower

Some propose that the mystery surrounding the performance and motivation of the charismatic's followers can be explained by the followers themselves. (See, for example, Downton, 1973; Kets de Vries, 1988.) They argue that only a certain type of person is attracted to a charismatic leader in the first place. These are people who are easily molded and persuaded by a strong leader because of their weak and dependent character. They are drawn to the charismatic leader because he exudes what they lack: self-confidence and conviction. They work hard to win his approval and earn his respect. In one study, "Moonies," the followers of a charismatic religious leader, the Reverend Sun Moon, had greater feelings of cynicism, helplessness, distrust of political action, and less confidence in their own sexual identity than a sample of average college students (Lodahl, 1982). In other studies, the followers of political and religious charismatics have been found to have less self-esteem, more experiences of psychological distress, and a higher intolerance for indecision and crisis than others. (See, for example, Davies, 1954; Freemesser and Kaplan, 1976; Galanter, 1982.)

Characteristics of dependency and poor self-esteem are not, however, uniformly found among the subordinates of charismatic business leaders. Many of the studies just described focused on followers who were disaffected by society, and none of them involved business organizations. In most business settings there is likely to be a broad range of individuals—from those who are assertive to those who are servile. Both types can become followers of charismatic leaders. In business organizations, subordinates often do not freely choose to follow a certain boss. More commonly the boss is hired or promoted into that position and the subordinates are already in place. So for subordinates there is often no freedom to select who will lead them—the weak do not always have the opportunity to gravitate to the strong. In turn, a leader may find himself inheriting a staff of confident, assertive subordinates. People may be drawn to entrepreneurial companies, for example, precisely because of the challenge and opportunity. They may be seeking the risk and uncertainty associated with new ventures—in contrast to employees described as dependent seekers of certainty. Clearly, then, some subordinates may be characterized by a strong sense of self-confidence.

Moreover, most studies of charismatic leaders have been conducted in crisis situations. In other words, the followers who were studied were needy by definition. While this may be the case with mature organizations in turmoil, entrepreneurial environments, as noted, are often filled with great excitement and stimulating challenges. It would therefore be wrong to assume that only the insecure will follow a charismatic leader. Charismatics can appeal to a wide range of people—some psychologically healthy, some not. Trying to find one universal set of followers' characteristics is the wrong avenue to an understanding of a charismatic's influence.

The Charismatic Relationship

There is agreement, however, on the effects of charismatic leaders on the behavior of followers. It often appears that much greater motivation and commitment characterize the subordinates of charismatic business leaders than others. In research studies, the subordinates of charismatics have been found to be more self-assured, work longer hours, find their work more meaningful, experience greater trust in their leaders, and have higher performance ratings than the followers of noncharismatic but effective leaders. (See Avolio and Bass, 1987; Howell, 1985; Smith, 1982; Yukl and Van Fleet, 1982.) Consistently, it has also been reported that followers will exhibit willing obedience to the leader, high trust in the leader and attachment to him, a sense of empowerment, and a greater sense of group cohesion around shared beliefs as well as less internal group conflict (Conger and Kanungo, 1988d; Yukl, 1989). These are rather remarkable findings. They also help explain why charismatic leaders are such powerful catalysts of change, given their ability to harness and direct a tremendous amount of human energy while at the same time ensuring commitment to themselves and their goals. But what is it specifically that the leader does throughout each of the four stages? (See Chapter Two.)

While little is known about the exact dynamics, there are two popular explanations. The first is based on Freudian theories of the ego. In this case, we return to the idea of the needy follower. Although I find this explanation inadequate, a brief review of the basic theory is in order. Until recently, this has been the accepted explanation for the power of charismatic leaders. According to Freudian theory, followers are striving to resolve a conflict between who they are and what they wish to become. They do this by substituting the leader as their ideal or, in Freudian terms, as the embodiment of their ego ideal (Downton, 1973). The leader, then, is the model for what they wish to become. The underlying assumption, however, is that followers are fulfilling a pathological need rather than a healthy desire for role models from whom to learn and grow.

Thus, for example, some psychoanalysts (Erikson, 1968; Downton, 1973) trace this need to *identity confusion*—a failure to mature in adolescence and young adulthood. Basically, certain people never develop an ideal self because of absent, weak, or oppressive parents. Identifying with the charismatic leader provides a means of coping with their own identity confusion and another chance for these people eventually to attain maturity. This dynamic causes followers to develop a strong emotional attraction to the leader and to comply with his or her wishes.

The second explanation, based on ideas from social psychologists and organizational researchers (see French and Raven, 1959; Kelman, 1958; House, 1977), seems more reasonable. In this case, followers are attracted to the leader because of their identification with his or her abilities. From personal observation, the process follows a typical pattern. The leader's qualities of strategic insight, unconventionality, dynamism, an ability to excite, and other traits appear so extraordinary that subordinates are naturally attracted to them. In some cases, they may actually be in awe of their leader. Think of working for Steven Jobs who at age twenty-nine built a billion-dollar company, Apple Computer. It is hard not to be impressed by his accomplishments and presence—especially if we recall from Chapter Five how successes and other positive impressions lead to perceptions of a one-of-a-kind leader. This extraordinary figure then becomes a model for success and excellence within their organization or, more generally, within their field of interest. The leader's qualities and skills become the yardstick against which subordinates measure their own performance. One subordinate captured the essence of this process in an interview: "Don is like a role model. You want to have that energy, both the physical and the intellectual. You want to have that tremendous insight—bam, just to see what he sees and have the ability to carry it out. I've grown tremendously. He's a teacher. You see what he has done, and you want to do it. You want to have the same impact."

Some subordinates even dream of acquiring the same power as their leader—of becoming charismatic leaders themselves. They come to believe that association with the leader will enable them to acquire some of his traits. A comment from a subordinate demonstrates this belief: "You want to be like your leader—it's hero worship. When you look at our boss, you ask yourself: 'Now why didn't I do that with such flamboyance?' We worship him because of the way that he did the common in an uncommon manner. We want to be able to do that—it's creative. I want to be like my idol so I can do it on my own. You have a basic need to learn from him. I wanted to learn. I wanted to be a good charismatic leader myself."

An organization's leader is often seen as the primary power figure. He becomes a model of how to succeed. Among subordinates, the desire arises, quite naturally, to emulate his strengths, his values. Subordinates want certain of the leader's qualities and values to ensure their own growth, success, and power within the organization. With charismatics, this process is intensified. I say *intensified* because this same experience occurs with other leaders but to a lesser degree—simply because noncharismatics are not often perceived as extraordinary nor do they necessarily go to the same extent of empowerment. None of the subordinates of the noncharismatics I interviewed described such a high degree of identification with their leader, for example. Thus identification with charismatic leadership is more a matter of degree than an either/or dichotomy. And while dependency and parent/child dynamics are indeed aspects of this identification, they can arise out of subordinates' constructive needs for growth rather than from the pathological motives suggested by some psychoanalysts.

Note, however, that identifying with the leader does not necessarily mean imitating the leader's behavior. It can mean simply internalizing his key values rather than copying his gestures and style (Bennis, Berlew, Schein, and Steele, 1973). Subordinates of charismatics sometimes acknowledge that they do not in fact wish to emulate their leader's behavior. Yet they may have internalized his values and ideology as their own. The following statement from the subordinate of a charismatic leader is typical: "There's a part of me that recognizes that I can't be him. However, I can and do take portions of his beliefs and values."

This identification process helps to explain why people are so attracted to such a leader in the first place. They learn to trust him because of his self-confidence, his strong convictions in the organization's mission, his willingness to undertake personal risk, and his history of accomplishment. Moreover, the leader may be continually using impression management techniques to reinforce his image of skill and ability. Part of the attraction, then, is a desire to share in the leader's values and skills and the positive outcomes associated with him. But this description falls short of fully explaining why the followers of charismatic leaders work so *hard* for them. Commitment and motivation are the result of several other forces besides identification.

As we saw in Chapters Three and Four, one of these forces involves the leader's vision. If his image of the future meets the aspirations of subordinates and presents an attractive outcome for their efforts, it can heighten their motivation. Recent research by Bernard Bass (1985) and his associate Bruce Avolio (Avolio and Bass, 1987) reveals that as a leader's vision appeals to subordinates' need for personal growth and self-realization, they are more likely to take on greater responsibility and work harder. As Steven Jobs describes the contribution that Next employees can make to revolutionizing education in their society, he offers them a way of meeting higher-order needs. In turn, he can expect a more highly motivated work force than if his vision met only their needs for job security and income. The vision's appeal is particularly important in mobilizing people with whom the charismatic leader has little or no direct interaction. For them, the leader's ability to make their mission one of great meaning and hope becomes a critical motivating factor. But even an attractive vision is itself insufficient to explain the exceptional motivation associated with charismatic leaders. Rather, the leader's relations with followers are the key.

What happens in a charismatic relationship? As subordinates identify more and more with their leader, they develop a certain dependency that can have positive or negative consequences. In either case, subordinates of charismatic leaders often describe the critical significance of their leader's *approval* as a source of confirmation. Indeed, it becomes the principal measure of their self-worth. Many subordinates report that it is their primary source of motivation:

> It's a challenge to earn Don's respect. That's why you do so well. It tells you how good you are, because he's so good. You're seeking Don's approval.

> You want to earn his respect because you respect him so highly—his intellect, his energy, his ability to get things done . . . it's a measure of how good you are . . . he is the premier marketer. You can imagine how important it is to have him say "That's right."

Because he is seen as such a desirable figure, people want his approval. The key reward is his approval.

This need for the leader's personal approval is also tied to the empowerment process described in Chapter Six. All along the way, the leader has been praising followers and making them feel special: "He can create enormous confidence in you. It's better than a raise. He just has this ability to make you feel very positive." This praise builds their confidence but also their sense of obligation to the leader. They develop more and more of a desire to live up to their leader's expectations—to continue to receive the praise they interpret as a confirmation of their abilities and self-worth. As the relationship grows, there is a deepening sense of obligation. The leader's confidence in subordinates creates a sense of duty and responsibility. Subordinates validate this trust through accomplishment. I have often heard statements like the following from subordinates of charismatic leaders: "Your motivation comes from the responsibility, authority, faith, and confidence that he has in you to get the job done. There is a sense of wanting to do exceptionally well because of the belief and responsibility that he has given you."

Into this process goes another element: high expectations and a sense of confidence in subordinates' abilities (House, 1977). Because charismatic leaders tend to have "big ideas," their visions are difficult to achieve and thus place exceptional demands on subordinates. So these leaders set high expectations and at the same time demonstrate confidence in their subordinates' ability to achieve them. The practice of empowerment is critical to encouraging and sustaining efforts to meet these demanding expectations. These two practices—setting high expectations and building confidence—are not unique to charismatic leaders, however, for I have found noncharismatics using similar tactics. What does appear to be different is the internal motivation for achieving goals. Again subordinates of charismatic leaders explain that they are motivated by the leader's approval to a far greater extent than by most other rewards.

The subordinates of charismatics feel they are fulfilling their potential as human beings when they meet their leader's high expectations. Their leader symbolizes such an extraordinary level of competence that successful subordinates believe that they too have achieved a state of excellence themselves. Indeed, a state of euphoria was often described at this moment.

The power of high expectations as a motivator sometimes appears to be tied to an element of precariousness created by emotional dependence on the charismatic leader. In interviews with subordinates I have often discerned a fear that their leader will withdraw his approval if they fail to meet his expectations. While the charismatic leader is actively empowering and building confidence, he can just as easily withdraw his support. This statement is typical: "You don't want to let him down. As a matter of fact, there's a fear that you're not going to be all that he wants you to be. That you'd not be part of the team—not worthy of being in the inner circle. It motivates you to do your best. It's really parenting. You want to be at his level."

This is an important clue to understanding the exceptional motivation and performance associated with charismatic leadership. The emotional bond is so strong that the subordinates' self-worth is defined by their association with the leader. Without it, subordinates feel as if they are underperforming and even failing. As well, they may feel a tremendous fear of becoming a member of the out-group. This quote from a subordinate of one particularly charismatic leader highlights the dilemma: "There's a love/hate element [in our relationship]. You love him when you're focused on the same issues. You hate him when the contract falls apart. Either you're part of the team or not—there's a low tolerance for spectators. And over a career, you're in and out. A lot depends on your effectiveness on the team. You have to build up a lot of credibility to regain any ground you've lost." So while the outward aspects of motivating may appear similar to those of other leaders (setting high expectations, expressing confidence, delegating difficult challenges), the critical difference with charismatic leadership is the degree to which the leader's personal approval becomes the supreme reward and sign of acceptance.

A final element that may help explain extraordinary performance is a sense of urgency conveyed by the leader. I have been repeatedly impressed by the high-pressure atmosphere that charismatic leaders tend to create around them. Subordinates may be led to believe that if they fail to meet certain deadlines, the mission itself will fail. These leaders, knowingly or not, create deadlines that place tremendous pressures on subordinates to achieve at high levels. Failing to do otherwise is interpreted as a threat to the mission's success and carries with it the possibility of falling from the leader's grace.

Returning to the idea of framing, an excerpt from a discussion between Steven Jobs and his staff members at Next captures this process of describing goals so that their urgent accomplishment becomes critical. In this case, Jobs is trying to frame a deadline for the shipment of the company's first computer. His management team is determined to keep the computer's price in an affordable range for students and professors ($3,000) and to bring the product to market by the summer of 1987. Jobs, however, is concerned that failure to have the product ready by summer 1987 could have serious implications for the company. He frames a specific belief about the impact of time on the mission and highlights the importance of their mission in light of this perception:

> *Crow:* If we really do believe that we have to ship this [computer] by summer of '87, then how are you going to move that up? I don't think price is going to change the schedule that much. I think the real risk is in the technology, it's not in the cost.
>
> *Barnes:* There's another option. You can go to the spring of '88.
>
> *Jobs:* Yes, we could. But the problem is if we do that . . . no, that's not the worst thing, the worst thing is the world isn't standing still, so by the spring of '88, well, we want color, and the technology window sort of passes us by, and all the work we've done we throw down the toilet and start over and, you know, since we've proved we can't do something great in eighteen months, why should we believe we could do it a year later? . . . I think we have to drive a stake in the

>   ground somewhere, and I think if we miss this win-
>   dow then a whole series of events come into play. We
>   can't sell enough units in '87 to pay for our operating
>   costs, word gets out that we're not doing that well, a
>   lot of the credibility starts to erode—I don't know,
>   you can make up all these fantasies, we've got to have
>   a stake in the ground.

Crow: The problem I've got, though, is, one, will everybody
>   believe the stake is in fact in the ground, and, two,
>   when Software comes back and says what they can
>   do by summer or spring of '87, will they be telling us
>   the truth. That's what I'm worried about. . . .

Jobs: Well, George, I can't change the world, you know.
>   What do you want me to do? What's the solution? I
>   don't want to hear just because we blew it last time,
>   we're going to blow it this time.
>
>   What I want is probably irrelevant. I mean there
>   are certain realities here, both psychological and mar-
>   ket, that are going to come into play, in my own per-
>   sonal judgment. And I think this is a window that
>   we've got. We've been given it, and thank God we've
>   been given it. Nobody else has done this. This is a
>   wonderful window. We have eighteen months! So I
>   don't think we have a company if we don't do this.
>   No matter what I say, or anybody else says, that is
>   my deepest belief: If we don't do this, we will not be
>   able to attract great people, we will not be able to re-
>   tain the ones, some of the ones we have, and, you
>   know, it just won't be us. [Nathan, 1986, pp. 9–10]

What Jobs does so skillfully here is to create a sense of
urgency that essentially demands greater performance from his
staff. He interprets reality—in this case the marketplace—as presenting a rare opportunity: "This is a wonderful window." He
creates the perception of a rare chance but one that is quickly
fleeting. In reality, this "window" may be greater than the time
span Jobs envisions. He raises the stakes by introducing the possibility of failure, perhaps in order to crank up the motivational

energy necessary to complete the project. He argues that failure of the company is the inevitable outcome if they miss the deadline: "So I don't think we have a company if we don't do this." According to Jobs, the market for his company's product depends on a single short-term time frame that must be met or else. In fact, Next did not make the deadline of mid-1987. The new computer was not unveiled until later, in 1988, and was not available for sale until mid-1989. Though the marketplace will be the ultimate judge of Jobs's "deadline," it seems fairly clear that no serious competition arose to produce a similar machine in the interim.

In summary, then, all these forces together create the dynamics of attraction, dependence, and performance associated with charismatic leaders. Through an appeal to higher-order needs, perceptions of extraordinary ability, expressions of approval, high expectations, empowerment, and a sense of urgency, the charismatic leader is able to forge a bond with followers that can result in commitment and performance quite beyond the ordinary. But a price may be paid for this achievement. For in this special relationship between the charismatic leader and the subordinate, a state of great dependency is often created. The subordinate's excessive dependence on the leader may cause certain problems unique to the charismatic leader. We will explore this dilemma, along with other problems associated with charismatic leaders, in Chapter Eight.

Chapter 8

The Dark Side of the Charismatic Leader

While we tend to think of the positive outcomes associated with charismatic leaders, there are certain risks associated with them as well. Management writer Peter Drucker went so far as to claim that "charisma becomes the undoing of leaders." While I do not hold such an extreme view, the very behavior that distinguishes charismatics from others can indeed produce problematic or even disastrous outcomes. When the charismatic leader's actions become too exaggerated, or lose touch with reality or his followers' needs, or become a means for pure personal gain, they may harm the leader and the organization itself. As a result, we need to examine the negative outcomes associated with these leaders and understand why they occur.

There are potential problems in each of the elements distinguishing charismatic leaders: in their vision, in their articulation of goals, and in the management practices they employ to achieve their visions. While some of these problems are common to many leaders, charismatic or not, we are likely to find more extreme forms among the charismatics. Given their ability to persuade, for example, they are more likely to secure continued commitment to failing goals than the average leader. As a result, negative outcomes could be more common under the charismatic leader. We begin, then, with the possible liabilities of the charismatic's vision.

Problems with the Leader's Vision

When strategic visions fail, the cause can usually be traced to the overwhelming intrusion of the leader's personal aims or to errors in perception. Charismatic leaders may substitute their personal goals for shared organizational goals, for example, constructing an organizational vision that is essentially a monument to themselves. Because such visions are driven by deep personal urges, they are unlikely to reflect the market's or the organization's needs. As a result, the vision may no longer represent a perspective shared by the organization's constituents. Thus the blind drive to create a uniquely personal vision can result in an inability to see problems and opportunities in the environment. Thomas Edison, for example, so passionately believed in the future of direct current for urban power grids that he failed to see the rapid acceptance of alternating-current systems by America's emerging utility companies. A company started by Edison to produce direct-current power stations was doomed to failure.

This personal monument-building syndrome is, I suspect, fairly typical of inventor-entrepreneurs like Edison. The inventor becomes so enamored with his own ideas and creations that he fails to see competing and ultimately more successful ideas. As well, such visions encourage the charismatic leader to expend enormous amounts of personal energy, passion, and resources on getting them off the ground. The greater his commitment, the less willing he is to see the viability of competing approaches. And because of the leader's commitment, the organization's investment is also likely to be far greater in such cases. Failure, therefore, will have more disastrous consequences.

The second cause of failed visions, errors in perception, may include an inability to detect fundamental changes in markets (competitive, technological, consumer needs), a failure to accurately assess and obtain the necessary resources for the vision's accomplishment, and a misreading of market demand or constituents' needs. At one point both John DeLorean and, to a lesser extent, Lee Iacocca wrongly believed that automobile style rather than engineering was the supreme and unchanging concern of automotive buyers. DeLorean tailored his DeLorean automobile around gull-wing doors and a shiny steel body rather than performance, reliability, and price. As a result, serious quality problems and a high price would later cause car sales to slump and contribute to the demise of DeLorean's company. At Chrysler, Iacocca relied on new body styles and his charisma to market cars built on an aging chassis (the K car) developed in the late 1970s. After several initial years of successful sales, Chrysler's sales plunged 22.8 percent in 1987 (Taylor, 1988, p. 79). Both leaders underestimated their market's desire for engineering quality. They failed to recognize fundamental changes that were occurring among American automobile buyers. While the 1960s and 1970s were the era of style, the 1980s were marked by a concern for quality and innovative engineering.

Ultimately, the success of a leader's vision depends upon a realistic assessment of both the opportunities and the constraints in the environment and a sensitivity to constituents' needs. If the leader loses sight of reality or loses touch with constituents, the vision itself may become a liability. Sometimes initial successes may breed in the leader a false belief in the vision's infallibility which ultimately results in its fallibility. While visions may fail for a wide variety of reasons, these are some of the significant ones:

- The leader's vision projects his personal needs rather than those of his market and constituents.
- The leader seriously miscalculates the resources needed to achieve his vision.
- The leader makes an unrealistic assessment or has a distorted perception of market demand and constituents' needs.
- The leader fails to recognize environmental changes and redirect his vision.

We will examine some of these categories by using illustrations of prominent business leaders.

Projection of Personal Needs. One of the most serious liabilities of charismatic leaders is their tendency to project purely
personal needs and beliefs onto those of their constituents. Typical is the inventor who has a great idea and acquires sufficient
resources to initiate a venture. But his idea must match the market's needs if the vision is ultimately to translate into a success.
If the leader's wishes diverge from those of his constituents,
there may be costly consequences. A good example of this is
Edwin Land, inventor of the Polaroid camera. Dr. Land's experiences with a camera he developed illustrate how a leader can get
sidetracked by his own personal goals (see Merry, 1976).

Land's company, Polaroid, held a monopoly on the instant photography market for some three decades and became
the household name for such cameras. Throughout the 1960s
and 1970s, Polaroid's sales climbed with astonishing speed. By
1973, four million of the company's Colorpack cameras were
being sold annually at $30 apiece. But Dr. Land was not con-
tent. His dream was to create what he called "absolute one-step
photography"—a concept embodied in a new camera called the
SX-70. "Photography will never be the same. . . . With the gar-
gantuan effort of bringing SX-70 into being, the company has
come fully of age," Land would remark on the day of the camera's inauguration.

In setting the parameters for his new vision, Land outlined several demanding criteria: The camera was to be totally
automatic, litter-free, fold to fit in a purse or pocket, possess a
single-lens reflex viewing system, and focus from less than a
foot to infinity. It was to be a radically new design, and Land
believed it would make earlier visions of instant photography in-
stantly obsolete.

The SX-70 also represented a major strategic shift for the
company. Before its advent, the manufacturing of Polaroid
products, especially films, was subcontracted to outsiders. Plant
and equipment were usually leased or rented. Land's dream for
the SX-70, however, required total integration of the company.
A color negative plant and camera assembly plant were designed
and built. The company's chemical production facilities and
film packaging were expanded.

Although the total cost of the SX-70 strategy was never

formally disclosed, Land responded in an interview that it was a half-billion-dollar investment. Other estimates have put it higher. In any case, the SX-70 was a design masterpiece—a $180 masterpiece. It was estimated that the reflex viewing system cost millions of dollars and required over two and a half years of engineering effort. The eyepiece alone cost $2 million in engineering.

Land's expectations of the camera's success were as lavish as his investment in the camera. At $180 per camera, company experts projected that first-year sales would reach several million units. By some accounts, five million units were predicted. Despite such optimism, the camera met with only limited public support. By the end of its first year in 1973, only 470,000 SX-70 cameras had been sold. It would take several years and many design changes and significant price cuts before the camera gained widespread market acceptance—all at the cost of sacrificing many of the camera's original features. For several reasons, Land's personal vision of the instant camera had missed what the market wanted.

In his quest for the perfect instant camera, he had above all failed to take into account lessons that his company had already learned about consumers' needs. Before the SX-70, Polaroid's experience with both its black-and-white and color cameras was that demand was intimately tied to price. Consumers wanted an inexpensive, easy-to-use, instant camera. Their foremost desire was not the perfect picture but an instant picture that was relatively good and at a low price. In the 1960s, the marketplace powerfully demonstrated its needs to Polaroid when the company first introduced its color system in 1963. It began with the Colorpack cameras priced at $100. Meeting with only limited market interest, Polaroid introduced a version at $75 and, by 1969, a $30 Colorpack. At the $30 price level, volume dramatically expanded, and four million units were sold by 1973. Consumers wanted instant photography but only at an inexpensive price. So how could five million SX-70s at $180 apiece be sold when only four million Colorpack cameras had been sold at $30 each? Clearly they could not. Dr. Land's vision was a personal ideal—one that was not shared by consumers at a price of $180 per camera.

Why had Land failed to learn from the past? There are

several explanations. Clearly his original vision of instant photography had been correct: People really did want instant photographs. This initial success, however, may have convinced Land of the invincibility of his ideas. Moreover, Land was an engineer at heart. He loved the technology more than the marketing of the product. By his very background, he was product and technology-oriented rather than market-oriented. He had been lucky in the sense that his inventions had coincided with the needs of the marketplace. Finally, and most important, I believe that Land, like other leaders, came to identify with his vision to an unhealthy extent. The vision personified himself. A similar example is Henry Ford. Ford was willing to build any color of Model T as long as it was black. The vision becomes so much of the leader's personality that he is unwilling or unable to consider contrary information from subordinates or from the marketplace. Convinced of his invincibility from past successes, he plows ahead without considering other viewpoints. At some point in his career, though, he will be wrong and failure will ensue.

Blind Ambition and Costly Miscalculations. In the quest to achieve a vision, the charismatic leader may be so driven as to ignore the costly implications of his strategic aims. Ambition and the miscalculation of necessary resources can lead to a "Pyrrhic victory" for the leader. The word *Pyrrhic* comes from the ancient Greek king of Epirus, Pyrrhus, who sustained heavy losses in his desire to defeat the Romans. Although he had numerous successes, the costs of his victories were so excessive that they later undermined his whole empire.

In this scenario, the charismatic leader is usually driven by the desire to expand or accelerate the realization of his vision. The initial vision appears correct, and early successes essentially delude or weaken the leader's ability to assess his resources and marketplace realities. The costs that must be paid for market share or entry into new markets ultimately become unsustainable and threaten the long-term viability of the leader's organization.

Donald Burr of People Express is an example of a Pyrrhic victor. With remarkable success, Burr had taken People Express from nothing in 1980 to a billion-dollar company by the end of

1985. *Venture* magazine described him as "an entrepreneurial legend" (Garrett, 1986, p. 102). But his initial successes would lead him to dangerously greater ambition. No longer content to conceive of People Express as a regional carrier, he began to envision a national and international airline.

In 1983, he acquired several Boeing 747 jets and initiated overseas discount flights from Newark, New Jersey, to London. In 1984, People Express added ten new airports. At the end of 1985, however, Burr made his most dramatic move—a $300 million acquisition of Frontier Airlines. It seemed an unusual opportunity to acquire established routes in the Western United States and a second hub in Denver linking People Express to more than a hundred airports with over six hundred flights daily. In Burr's mind, the Frontier acquisition also opened up opportunities to use profits from one region in order to slash fares in another and steal market share from competitors (Byrne, 1985, p. 81).

But competitors quickly responded with their own fare cuts. The effects of these retaliatory moves soon appeared on People's balance sheet. By the end of 1985, People Express was losing $27.5 million. Burr's "victories" in expansion were taking their toll in human resources, as well. Nearly 20 percent of the company's pilots departed, along with 15 percent of its flight attendants and four managing officers (Garrett, 1986). There was growing disenchantment among employees. The company's dramatic growth was outstripping its ability to maintain a humanistic orientation. As well, its stock price dropped from a 1983 high of $25 to below $20 at the end of 1985. For employees, the stock-ownership program—a keystone of its humanistic orientation—was losing its luster.

Burr's leadership style began to change. As *Business Week* noted in November 1985: "Burr got tough. He froze salaries and hiring. . . . Burr's enlightened manager-owner work force grew disenchanted." He would also become more defensive and more authoritarian as he increasingly lost control. "Leadership," he announced, "is not pandering to what people say they need. It's defining what the hell people need. It's not saying 'Oh yeah, you want another candy bar? Here, rot your teeth.' That's not what builds empires. . . . All I want to do is win" (Byrne, 1985). His quest for greater market victories would cause him to lose touch with his own organization's needs. "We lost our sense of family and gained a sense of alienation," said one customer service manager to a reporter.

By the end of the first quarter of 1986, People Express's losses totaled $58 million. At the same time, the company went on to acquire two commuter airlines! By the summer, losses had reached staggering proportions of over $100 million. Both *Fortune* and *Business Week* carried headlines of the airline's plunge and speculated that People Express or parts of it would soon be sold. In the face of rapidly accelerating losses, Burr surprisingly shifted People's strategy from a no-frills airline to one that offered complimentary baggage check-in, first-class service, and free meals. Higher fares, of course, accompanied these changes. His game plan now was to recoup losses by appealing to a broader spectrum of travelers other than seasonal ones, but in doing so his airline lost its uniqueness. Ultimately, this change in strategy would cause a drop in the airline's load factor to 56 percent by May 1986 and 45 percent by June—normally busy travel periods. The about-face in vision cost Burr dearly. In his panic over financial conditions, he had abandoned the company's distinctive strength.

Sensing that higher prices were not working, he returned to his original strategy of discount fares. But time had run out. Net income losses reached $160 million, and the company's share price dropped to $4. By September 1986, People Express was nearly insolvent, and Frontier was in Chapter 11 bankruptcy proceedings. On September 15, Frank Lorenzo, chairman of Texas Air Corporation, acquired People Express for $300 million in stock, notes, and a small amount of cash. The airline had come quite cheaply. Burr's victories had ended in the merger of People Express with Texas Air. His empire was now another man's.

Burr's tragic error is tied as much to blind ambition as it is to poor strategic decisions. In this case, the charismatic leader senses his initial strategy is correct. There is a good deal of market success in the early stages. This, however, in combination with an ambitious personality, leads the visionary to dream of ever greater expansion. The idea of an empire becomes more important than the satisfaction of enjoying one's present success. The leader then undertakes ever more ambitious strategies—failing to see that he may not possess the long-term resources necessary to sustain his grand plan, especially if he underestimates the response of competitors. Wishing to maintain an image of self-confidence, the leader dismisses these problems and steadfastly maintains his commitment to failing operations. As he senses a loss of control over the well-being of his organization, his style becomes ever more autocratic. As he exerts greater and greater control, he becomes less able to hear the counsel of others that might be helpful. In the worst case, the organization's resources are exhausted and the company fails.

Exaggerated Perceptions. Sometimes the leader's perceptions of a market are greatly exaggerated or so significantly ahead of their time that the marketplace fails to sustain the venture. The organization's resources are mobilized and spent on a mission that ultimately does not produce the expected results. In this case, the leader is perhaps too visionary. He is unable to see that the time is not ripe, and the vision marches on to failure or, at best, a long dormancy period.

Robert Lipp, former president of Chemical Bank, is an example of a visionary charismatic who in one project was essentially too far ahead of his time. In the early 1980s he championed a vision of home banking. Sensing that the personal computer was revolutionizing many aspects of everyday life, Lipp and others at Chemical Bank suspected that personal banking itself would be the next beneficiary of the PC revolution. Through a modem, a phone line, software supplied by the bank, and a personal computer at home, people could instruct their banks to carry out certain transactions. A service fee of $8 to $15 a month was charged for personal users and $20 to $50 a month for small businesses.

From the user's viewpoint, home banking provided the convenience of bill paying and the ease of access to accounts. While on trips away from home, the user could instruct the system to pay bills on exact due dates. For banks, too, electronic

home banking was very appealing. The cost of printing, processing, and returning some forty-one billion checks annually in the
United States amounted to $41 billion (Sigel, 1986, p. 128).
This figure represented 20 percent of the annual revenues of
banks belonging to the Federal Reserve system. Home banking
offered the possibility of a tremendous reduction in operating
costs.

In 1983, Chemical Bank under Lipp's guidance introduced
a home banking system called the Pronto Two with a goal of
four million customers within several years. By 1988, however,
the total number of users of home banking systems nationwide
had reached only 100,000 people. *Business Week* (Zinn, 1988,
p. 109) remarked: "When Chemical Bank unveiled the idea of
home banking in 1983, it projected that 10% of its customers
would eventually pay bills and make banking transactions from
their home computer. Talk about misplaced optimism. Today,
if you're among those who deal with any bank by personal
computer, you're in a minority of a mere 100,000 people—and
that includes a number of small business operators." Only thirty
banks were offering the service by 1988, out of a total of four-
teen thousand banks nationwide.

What Chemical and others later discovered was that there
were several inherent problems with home banking systems that
met with consumer resistance. First, customers were reluctant
to give up the "float" between when they wrote a check and
when it was actually cashed. With home banking, once a payment is authorized by the computer it is immediately debited
from the customer's account, unlike a check. Second, some investment was required on the customer's part for a computer
and modem. It is estimated that only 10 percent of personal
computer owners had modems. Moreover, there were only a
limited number of personal computers in homes. Finally, it was
a matter of opinion whether writing a paper check was not just
as simple and convenient as paying bills on a personal computer.

Given the costs associated with such systems, it was believed that only by providing a wider range of services such as
home shopping services would home banking's appeal increase.
A senior banker commented that the system "must work its

way insidiously into the marketplace" over a period of ten to fifteen years and had to be packaged with additional home information and transaction services in order to reach the consumer market (Sigel, 1986).

In Lipp's case, his vision was essentially premature for its market. Part of the problem could be attributed to the difficulty of trying to predict a future event. And when there is no precedent, it is especially hard to estimate the demand for a particular product or service. The leader is essentially relying on his interpretation of market trends and his own resources. The margin of error in these situations is exceptionally high. As well, the costs and time horizons for introducing a new product or service are often underestimated. Such miscalculations can forestall a vision.

Two other factors may also play important roles. Leaders in their own excitement over an idea may fail to test-market a new product or service adequately or fail to hear nay-sayers. Again, because of successes in other projects, they may delude themselves into believing they know their markets better than they actually do. Or they may not be adept at interpreting marketplace trends yet are sufficient spellbinders to lead.

Failure to Recognize Flaws. All three of these cases share certain characteristics in common that cause charismatic and other leaders to deny the flaws in their visions. Often a leader will perceive that his course of action is producing negative results, yet he persists. Why this happens can be explained by a process called cognitive dissonance (see Festinger, 1957) that prevents the leader from changing his course. Simply put, people keep the commitments they have made because failing to do so would damage favorable perceptions of themselves. Studies have found, for example, that executives sometimes persist in an ineffective course of action only because they feel they have committed themselves to the decision. In one study, decision makers allocated greater sums of money to money-losing divisions than to profitable ones, especially if they were originally responsible for supporting the ineffective division (Steers, 1984; Staw, 1976; Staw and Ross, 1978). These executives did not wish to admit that their decision had been in error and so continued to support the money-losing ventures. This same process, I suspect, occurs with charismatic leaders. Thus we find Donald Burr months before the disappearance of People Express into Texas Air stating: "These dire stories about a cataclysmic collapse are all out of proportion" (Norman, 1986, p. 31). Thus we find one executive of DeLorean's ill-fated automobile adventure admitting: "I was hooked. At a certain point I got too many of my friends involved as investors, dealers, and employees. I couldn't let them down and just back out" (Levin, 1983, p. 241).

Because subordinates tend to become dependent on such leaders, they may perpetuate the problem by their own actions. They may lionize their leader, for example, and in turn ignore his dark side while exaggerating his virtues. As a result, subordinates may unquestioningly carry out their leader's orders. Because of their great need to dominate and be admired, leaders may even encourage such behavior. The danger is that a leader will surround himself with yes-men and fail to receive information that might be important but challenging to the mission. Because of their subordinates' admiration, leaders may believe themselves to be as powerful or intelligent as others think. A sense of omnipotence then leads to denying market and organizational realities.

Finally, groupthink (Janis, 1972) can result if the leader's advisers seduce themselves into agreement with him. In such a case, decision making becomes distorted and a thorough review of solutions is all but precluded. This is especially true of groups that are cohesive, highly committed to their success, under pressure, and self-confident—common characteristics of the organizations of charismatic leaders. When groupthink occurs, the opinions of the leader and likeminded advisers come to dominate decision making. Doubts are kept hidden for fear of disapproval. It is more important "to go along to get along" than to consider contrary viewpoints.

One of the more renowned charismatic political leaders, John F. Kennedy, is often cited in examples of groupthink. His decision, along with other members of his cabinet, to go ahead with the CIA's planned invasion of Cuba in 1961 shows the disastrous impact of such decision-making processes. His plan called for a strike force of Cuban exiles combined with U.S. Air Force and Navy assistance to land at the Bay of Pigs in Cuba. This invasion force was then expected to spark a rebellion against Castro's communist government. Kennedy and several of his advisers were so committed to the project that other aides were reluctant to offer their dissenting views during the final decision. The decision was made, and the results were calamitous. After three days of fighting, the exiles were defeated and the rebellion never materialized. The advisers who foresaw these consequences had chosen not to speak but instead went along with the group.

John DeLorean is another leader who may have purposely created groupthink situations. One executive dismissed by DeLorean from the company board commented: "He told me he knew how some of the things the board was doing bothered my conscience. He said he wanted me to keep a clear conscience and not to worry as much as I did, so he had dropped me from the board. . . . He couldn't bear having anyone disagree with him, so he had to stack the board his way. John just nodded and said, 'That's right. It's my company and I'm going to do what I want to do—when you get your own company, you can do the same' " (Levin, 1983, p. 248).

Manipulation Through Communication Skills

Because of their gift at communicating, it is quite easy for charismatic leaders to misuse this ability. For instance, they may present information that makes their visions appear more realistic or more appealing than they actually are. They may also use their language skills to screen out problems in the environment or to foster an illusion of control when, in reality, things are quite out of control. Among their most grievous acts in this regard are:

- Exaggerated self-descriptions
- Exaggerated claims for their vision
- Fulfilling images of uniqueness in order to manipulate audiences

- Gaining commitment by suppressing negative information and publicizing positive information
- Using positive anecdotes to distract attention away from negative facts
- Creating an illusion of control through affirming information and attributing failure to external causes

John DeLorean was particularly adept at using his skills of articulation and impression management to promote himself. He would often claim responsibility for projects without acknowledging the contributions of others, for example (Levin, 1983). His aim was simply to manipulate information so that *he* appeared as the originating genius. In the case of the highly successful Pontiac GTO, DeLorean claimed to be the engineer at Pontiac who conceived the idea of combining a lighter version of the Tempest body with a powerful engine to create the GTO. In reality, the idea was suggested by a GM colleague. In *Current Biography*, DeLorean is described as owning "more than two hundred patents, including those for the recessed windshield wipers and the overhead-cam engine." A biographer, however, reported that the U.S. Patent Office listed a total of fifty-two patents for DeLorean, none for the wipers or overhead cam (Levin, 1983). Exaggerating his personal deeds was DeLorean's way of building the legend.

One biographer of Steven Jobs reported statements made by an Apple employee, Jef Raskin, who claims to be the originator of the MacIntosh computer: "I was the one who put it all together, but Jobs told everyone that he had done it. It took me two years to negotiate that deal with Xerox" (Bucher, 1988, p. 136). Thus we see that with some charismatic leaders the need for personal recognition is so great that they may distort reality to enhance their own image.

Because charismatic leaders rely so extensively on their impression management skills in communicating, they run a special risk. Research on impression management suggests that one's self-descriptions are not only effective in deceiving an audience but may deceive the presenter as well—especially when the audience approves of the figure's image (Schlenker, 1980).

As a result, the leader may come to believe he is as great as he claims. There are, however, limits to such effects. Those who blatantly exaggerate their self-image beyond the bounds of possibility do not tend to internalize their self-enhancing claims. When it comes to moderate exaggeration, however, people do tend to internalize and believe their claims. Thus DeLorean may ultimately have come to believe in his own responsibility for the Pontiac GTO.

As well, considerable research has been performed on people who are ingratiators—individuals who play to their audience by providing them with what they wish to hear. Charismatic leaders in particular use two tactics to ingratiate their audiences: fulfilling stereotypes and creating an image of uniqueness. If charismatic figures behave in ways that fulfill the positive stereotypes of an audience, they are more likely to have successful interactions with it (Goffman, 1959). They can do so by espousing the beliefs, values, and behavior associated with the stereotype and by appearing just as the stereotype is expected to look. John DeLorean supposedly went to great lengths to fulfill the image of a young, highly successful executive with an entrepreneurial spirit. He underwent cosmetic surgery, dieted from 200 pounds to 160, lifted weights, dyed his gray hair black. He flew only first class. When he ate out, he always obtained the best table (Levin, 1983, p. 155). He even married a model. To many, his image fulfilled the stereotype of the successful businessman. Mary Kay always appears carefully made up and beautifully dressed. After his rise to prominence, Lee Iacocca began to appear in European-styled double-breasted suits with a cigar in hand.

The second tactic is to demonstrate uniqueness. DeLorean achieved this effect through his tales of innovation at General Motors as well as by his unconventional actions while working at the automobile giant. These stories created the image of a highly successful yet unique individual excelling in the corporate world. But this uniqueness strategy must be balanced. If the figure is too unusual, he will be perceived as too deviant and fail to develop rapport.

In terms of how or what a leader communicates, there are

several tactics they can use to gain commitment from others even under unethical circumstances. Because of our limited ability to process vast streams of information, we rely on simple biases as well as rules of thumb to reduce the amount of information we need to make a decision. Through these biases and heuristics, leaders can stimulate commitment to a certain course of action. A leader can restrict information that is not favorable to his cause, for example, while providing more positive information. As noted earlier in discussing the greater impact of anecdotal information over statistical information, a leader can bias his audience's perceptions through the effects of stories. Especially when anecdotal information is consistent, it may discourage decision makers from searching for other information.

John DeLorean's management of investors in his automobile venture is but one example of this process. If investors had looked carefully they would have found that the odds of DeLorean succeeding were slim. Not since the founding days of the four major auto companies had a new automobile company succeeded—and there had been many attempts. As well, there was negative information in the company prospectus that might have dissuaded investors. But investors chose not to focus on the facts; their attention was on DeLorean's personal character (Schwenk, 1986). It would seem that DeLorean created an image in the minds of investors aimed at reducing their motivation to search out and use other sources of information: "For DeLorean, the impressive stack of press clippings was a potent weapon. No other entrepreneur in business history used publicity as well in amassing his seed capital, and he found that investors were as unlikely to look behind his hollow hype as reporters. . . . DeLorean underwent only the most cursory check into his background before he was loaned hundreds of millions of dollars" (Levin, 1983, p. 323).

Anecdotal information may be used by the charismatic leader not only to influence decision makers' choices but also to influence their confidence in a choice. The *amount* of information that the leader provides may build overconfidence. According to various studies of decision making (see Dreman, 1979; Oskamp, 1962), getting more information apparently permits people to marshal more reasons for justifying their decisions and, in turn, increases their confidence.

Leaders can also create an illusion of control by selectively providing information that affirms they are in control and attributes problems to external causes. In annual reports, for example, executives often use their letters to shareholders to claim responsibility for successes while blaming external forces for problems (Salancik and Meindle, 1984). By providing information that allows supporters to attribute failure to external causes or to ignore information about the true costs of a choice, a leader can mobilize continued support for a faltering mission. By encouraging supporters to make public statements of commitment, they may come to feel personally responsible for their initial commitment and therefore persist (Staw, 1976, 1981). All of these tactics may be used by the charismatic leader to mislead subordinates and investors.

Dysfunctional Management Practices

The management practices of charismatic leaders may have certain inherent liabilities, as well. Some of these leaders are known to be excessively impulsive and autocratic in their management style. Others are so disruptive in their unconventional behavior that their organizations mobilize against them. Moreover, they can at times be poor managers of relations with peers and superiors. In many cases, some of the very management practices that make these leaders unique are also responsible for their downfall. Problems fall into several categories: their relations with powerful others, their management style with subordinates, and their attention to administrative detail. Associated with each of these categories is a constellation of typical problems:

- Poor management of people networks (especially superiors)
- Unconventional behavior that alienates
- Creation of in-group/out-group rivalries that disrupt the organization
- Autocratic management style

- Impulsive style that is disruptive and dysfunctional
- Alternating between idealizing and devaluing others (especially subordinates)
- Empowerment creating excessive dependence
- Failure to manage details effectively
- Obsession with the superficial
- Absence from operations
- Failure to develop successors of equal ability

We will start with the first category—managing relations with others.

Managing Others. Certain charismatic leaders are very poor at managing peers and superiors. This, of course, applies principally to charismatics in large organizations. Because they are usually unconventional advocates of radical reform, they may often alienate other parts of their organization—including their own bosses. Arch McGill's brash, aggressive style may have alienated many potential supporters and ultimately left him without sufficient political backing during the restructuring of AT&T. This is a characteristic problem when a charismatic leader is brought in from the outside. The leader's radical approach may alienate the rest of the organization.

A similar situation arose at General Motors when Ross Perot was made a board member. Once on the board, Perot became one of the company's most outspoken critics. Quite naturally, as an entrepreneur, he was accustomed to running his own show. After his company Electronic Data Systems (EDS) merged with GM, he insisted that any changes made in EDS's procedures be cleared through him. His outspoken style so alienated the gentleman's culture at GM that the company offered Perot $700 million in stock to step down from the board—an offer he finally accepted.

A second problem related to managing relations in large organizations is the tendency of many charismatics to cultivate a sense of specialness among members of their operating unit. This practice is often accompanied by a corresponding depreciation of other parts of the corporation. An "us versus them" attitude is created. While heightening the motivation of the charismatic's group, it further alienates other groups that may be important for resources or political support. Steven Jobs did this with the Macintosh division at Apple Computer. Although the company's Apple II computer provided the profits, Jobs consistently downplayed that division's importance. Essentially he divided the company into two rivals. He was fond of telling people in the Macintosh division, "This is the cream of Apple. This is the future of Apple" (Bucher, 1988, p. 139). He even went so far as to tell marketing managers for Apple II that they worked for an outdated clumsy organization (p. 180). Jobs's later departure from Apple was to some extent tied to morale problems he created within the company by using this tactic. John DeLorean, of course, is notorious for his countercultural management practices that offended General Motors's management.

In another case the charismatic president of a division of a large corporation used a mascot symbol of a TV cartoon character, the Roadrunner, for his group. He had seen television cartoons of this wily creature outwitting a coyote again and again. His division managers, he thought, were the "roadrunners" who were smarter and faster than the corporate "coyotes" who laid roadblocks in their path. When corporate staff requested reports or information, he would ignore them or return the reports with the words "STUPID IDEA" stamped on the front cover. Such tactics, while fostering a sense of camaraderie and aggressiveness within the charismatic's division, were ultimately detrimental for both the charismatic and the overall organization. In this case, like Arch McGill, the executive eventually departed.

Relations with Subordinates. Troubling supervisory problems are occasionally associated with the management style of charismatic leaders. Some have been described as exceptionally autocratic. When People Express started to plunge, Donald Burr became more and more controlling. Steven Jobs has been described as dictatorial (Bucher, 1988). In many cases the leader's vision is such a personification of himself that he becomes obsessed with its achievement. Impatience with the pace of the achievement exacerbates the problem and encourages the charismatic to be even more controlling. As well, at times there appears to be an impulsive dynamic—especially in relation to accomplishing the vision.

John DeLorean is described as increasing production of the DeLorean car by 50 percent in the belief that his product would be an overnight sensation. So production went to an annual rate of thirty thousand cars—despite market research that showed total annual sales of four to ten thousand units. A company executive lamented: "Our figures showed that this was a viable company with half the production. If the extravagance had been cut out of New York, we could have broken even making just six thousand cars a year. But that wasn't fast enough for John. First he had to build his paper empire in the stock market. A creditable success was not enough for him" (Levin, 1983, p. 282). Steven Jobs is known to have caused havoc by darting in and out of operations: "He would leap-frog back and forth among various projects, dictating designs, with little or no knowledge of whether or not the technology even existed to make his ideas work" (Bucher, 1988, pp. 140–141).

Using an informal style to manage the hierarchy of an organization can also lead to problems. The advantage of this style is that the charismatic is approachable and can quickly react to issues and problems. The drawback is that charismatics often violate the chain of command by going around subordinates and in turn lessening the authority of their subordinates. If a certain project interests them, they do not hesitate to become involved, sometimes to the detriment of the project manager's responsibilities. John DeLorean would drop in on his engineers to suggest what seemed trivial ideas. One company engineer said: "He came in one day to say we should hook into the cooling system and make a little icebox for a six-pack of beer behind the driver's seat. Or, another time, he told us to work on a sixty-watt radio speaker that could be detached and hung outside the car for picnics" (Levin, 1983, p. 267).

Some charismatics will idealize subordinates and then later devalue them in what might be called the "golden boy" or "golden girl" syndrome. Typically a bright, young member of the management team is hand-picked by the charismatic for special projects and then, in time, is assigned to increasingly tougher

assignments. As long as he succeeds, the leader appears to idealize him. Eventually, however, he reaches a point where the task
exceeds his abilities and then he encounters serious problems.
At this point, he appears to fall from the leader's grace and is
soon replaced by another "golden boy." I have witnessed this
process with two charismatic leaders. (See also Kets de Vries
and Miller, 1984.)

Finally, subordinates can become addicted to their leader's empowerment. The charismatic becomes the "quick fix"
for feeling good about themselves. The trouble is that some subordinates have described this experience as an emotional roller
coaster. One minute they feel loved and respected; the next
minute they feel unworthy. Clearly this dynamic creates an unhealthy dependency. As well, the charismatic empowers subordinates so they can achieve difficult tasks. But what if these
tasks lead to disaster? Believing in their leader's faith and convictions, followers may simply escalate their commitment to
tasks that are doomed.

Administrative Skills. Some charismatic leaders are so absorbed in the big picture that they fail to understand essential
details—except for pet projects, in which case they become excessively involved. Lee Iacocca, for instance, turned over most
of the day-to-day operations to others as he became increasingly
famous and as a result lost touch with new model planning. He
himself admitted: "If I made one mistake, it was delegating all
the product development and not going to a single meeting"
(Taylor, 1988, p. 81). A DeLorean executive complained: "[John
DeLorean] just didn't have time for the details of the project.
But attention to detail is everything" (Levin, 1983, p. 267). As
well, charismatics may get so caught up in corporate stardom
that they become absentee leaders. Again, Lee Iacocca is an example. His success at Chrysler led to his becoming a best-selling
author, a U.S. presidential prospect, and the head of the $277
million fund-raising campaign for the Statue of Liberty—all of
which distracted him from the task of leading Chrysler.

Because these figures are often excited by ideas, they
may at times be poor implementers. Once an idea begins to
translate into reality, they sometimes feel the need to move on

to the next challenge, leaving subordinates scrambling to pick up the pieces. As well, because many charismatics seem to have a great need for visibility, they gravitate toward activities that afford them widespread recognition. Such activities rarely involve sitting at a desk paying careful attention to details.

Succession Problems. The charismatic leader is a strong figure and, as noted, often one who develops dependent subordinates. As such, it is difficult for employees with leadership potential to develop fully in the shadow of such leaders. For while charismatics do coach their subordinates, the latter are not likely to develop into leaders of equal power. The charismatic leader is simply too fond of the limelight to share it. When ultimately the charismatic departs, a leadership vacuum is created. Trice and Beyer (1986) tell the story of the charismatic founder of the National Council on Alcoholism (NCA). As executive director for over a quarter of a century, she essentially dominated all of the organization's developments. When she departed, there was no one as skilled and knowledgeable in administering the organization. Subsequently, NCA experienced infighting and had trouble maintaining the support of its members.

In conclusion, then, many of the charismatic's qualities have both a positive and a negative face. As such, the presence of a charismatic leader entails risks for his subordinates, his organization, and at times even his society. The negatives, however, must always be weighed in light of the positives. In large companies, the need for organizational change may be so great that they are willing to pay the price of confrontation, unconventionality, and all the rest. But it may also be possible to train, socialize, and manage future leaders so that the charismatic's drawbacks can be minimized. We will examine these issues in Chapter Nine.

Chapter 9

Developing Exceptional Leadership in Organizations

Charismatic leaders present a paradox for organizations: Their very strengths are also their potential weaknesses. It is as if we cannot live without them, and we cannot live with them. They offer us the best of outcomes and the worst of outcomes. But the issue is, in reality, not so black and white. For while there is a dark side, there may be ways to control its expression. More significant, the skills of the charismatic leader in communicating, in motivating, and in innovating are so vitally important that we cannot dismiss these leaders as fascinating curiosities. Simply recall a number of the revolutionary products and services that under their leadership have become commercial realities—the instant camera, the personal computer, overnight package delivery, data processing tools, cars such as the Mustang, and so on. Think of the major organizations they have revitalized—like Chrysler or Scandinavian Airlines or Chemical Bank's retail operations—organizations employing tens of thousands. Nor should we forget the confidence and self-esteem they have instilled in their workers—such as Mary Kay's industrious cadre of housewives. Wherever they have been, a legacy of value is usually left behind. Even Arch McGill is remembered for the changes he brought to marketing at AT&T—changes that helped carry the company into a new era of deregulation and competition. These innovative leaders and their skills are far too important to ignore. Even with their shortcomings, we need them.

What, then, can we do to maximize their effectiveness? How can their qualities be learned and developed? How can we select, train, and manage charismatic leaders to ensure the vitality of our mature organizations and the flourishing of entrepreneurship? These are a few of the issues we must address in this final chapter. To do so, we will have to shift our focus and take a more pragmatic perspective toward the central question: What are the *implications* of charismatic leadership for organizations and for managers?

We begin, then, with the most controversial issue: Can we actually train and develop charismatic leadership? While there may be training companies offering "charisma workshops" or seminars entitled "Charisma: How to Get It, How to Use It," little is being done to train charismatic leadership. This is probably just as well. When charisma is reduced to an "essence" that you and I can buy and sell like an enticing cologne, it has already lost its power. My approach is rather different. Above all, I think you *can* teach much of the behavior I have been discussing. Whether one will become a charismatic leader as a result of such training is another issue.

In the first place, it is debatable whether everyone can become charismatic. Some of us simply do not possess enough of the basic skills or the cognitive orientation to think and act like a charismatic leader. A lot of us may not have the *motivation* to be a charismatic leader or, for that matter, to lead. Even with motivated individuals, too many of these leaders in one organization might create chaos and bitter infighting. As well, charisma is a relational phenomenon as we have seen throughout this book. Such dynamics are not easily duplicated à la cookbook style. It takes time and certain skills and values for this relationship to emerge. Finally, although we may not want a charismatic leader in our organization, we may want more effective strategy or communication skills.

It might be more useful, therefore, to approach the issue of training charismatic leadership not from the perspective of creating an army of charismatic leaders but rather with the goal of enhancing the general leadership skills of our managers. So we might draw lessons from the strategy skills of charismatic leaders to enhance a manager's strategic abilities—in other words, use these leaders as teachers in the areas where we feel our managers are weakest. Charismatic leadership then becomes one of a variety of means to help us develop an individual's leadership. In the next section we look at the general issue of leadership training.

Developing Leaders

The great management tragedy today is the lack of leadership in many of our organizations. Because of the scarcity of good leadership, most of us assume it is something only a few figures can possibly possess. Yet the potential to lead lies dormant in many more of our managers than we realize. Leadership is not some magical ability limited to a handful. Rather the ability and desire to lead are often lost because of a lack of opportunity and little investment in the processes and rewards that foster its growth. It is a matter, then, of tapping, developing, and encouraging these dormant abilities. Many organizations, however, often do the opposite and actively discourage leadership skills by their benign neglect and concern for "managing" and for preserving the status quo. The price they pay is a great deal of lost leadership potential and, in turn, organizational effectiveness that is never realized.

The problem is also a matter of where we have focused our energies in developing leaders. Companies and government agencies have devoted much of their energy to training programs—typically offering simple leadership models with feedback sessions to provide managers with greater self-awareness on a series of "leadership" dimensions. This approach has serious flaws. First, what many training programs call leadership is in reality "managership." These programs have in essence perpetuated administrative skills rather than leadership skills. They teach simple goal setting, managing by objectives, participative decision making, and so on—skills of a much different nature than those described in this book. And while these skills are vital to effective managership, other capacities are more critical to effective leading such as vision, persuasive abilities, motivational skills, and so on.

The second problem with current approaches to developing leadership is that many stop with the training program. It is assumed that a week-long session on leadership will turn someone into a leader. This of course is nonsense. To develop a leader takes more than a training program. It is an important step, but only one of many. Instead companies must begin leadership development at the very moment of recruiting. Thereafter job experiences, rewards, the company culture, organizational structures, and training must all work together to reinforce and promote the skills of leading. The organization itself must in its actions encourage expressions of leadership. This is no simple task. For as our knowledge of leadership grows in sophistication, so must our steps to develop leaders. Companies must take a more integrated, life-long approach if they are to begin tapping the potential of today's managers. They must use the many experiences a manager faces in his or her career as opportunities to train and promote leadership.

Finally, our present approaches to leadership development fail to see that part of the problem is tied to our business culture and to our educational system. While famous for its creativity and vision in the entrepreneurial sector, our business culture is woefully unsupportive of these qualities in large corporations. Though this attitude is changing, thanks to fierce competitive pressures, there is still limited awareness of the need for managers to develop greater strategic powers, to become more effective communicators, to enhance their motivational skills, and to master the processes of organizational change and renewal. Corporations must actively encourage and reward these skills if they want them. Instead trainees returning from the company's once-a-year leadership seminar find themselves, not so surprisingly, returning to an office where opportunities to practice their new leading skills are rare and their initiatives go unrewarded.

Our business schools and, for that matter, even our undergraduate programs are also part of the problem. In some ways, we are failing to train young people in the very subjects that may later help them to think more creatively and comprehend the broad implications of market trends—topics in the social sciences and humanities, for example. To illustrate the predicament and, at the same time offer us a glimmer of hope that we can teach the creative skills of the charismatic leader, we turn now to the results of an unusual research study conducted at Carnegie-Mellon University a number of years ago. It suggests how it is possible to learn and unlearn skills such as imagination through coursework (Leavitt, 1986).

Bob Altemeyer, a Carnegie-Mellon researcher, decided to test two groups of students over their four years of college to see if they would develop different styles of thinking. One group was selected from the College of Fine Arts where they majored in architecture, art, design, or music; the other group was from the College of Engineering and Science where they majored in engineering, math, or the hard sciences. Carefully matched samples of freshmen, sophomores, juniors, and seniors were tested for analytic and logic skills and for imagination and intuition skills. Some of the results were surprising. But first, the not-so-surprising results. The engineering and science students significantly improved their scores on the analytic tests between freshman and senior years. The fine arts students significantly improved their scores, as well, but on imagination.

Now, however, the surprise. On tests measuring imagination, the engineering and science students showed a consistent *decrease in imagination* from the freshman year to the sophomore year and so on to the senior year. Their scores actually worsened. The fine arts students showed the same decline but in their analytic skills: While seniors scored significantly higher on tests of imagination than freshmen, they scored significantly lower on the analytic tests. Four years of education in the fine arts had improved imaginative thinking but with a loss in analytic problem-solving skills, while education in engineering had improved proficiency in analytic ability but at the cost of imagination. The learning of one style of thinking, it appears, may cause the active unlearning of the other (Altemeyer, 1966).

While these findings illustrate the power that education plays in either promoting or inhibiting certain abilities, they also seem to say that we can actively train and teach such skills. On this note of optimism, let us take a look at each of the skill areas of the charismatic leaders to see what possibly can be taught and developed.

Visioning Skills. In Chapter Three I described how the process of visioning was strongly linked to the leader's personal experiences and certain cognitive abilities. While we may not be able to train vision per se, we can certainly facilitate the processes that enable it to occur. Organizations can do this through four means: selection procedures, job experiences, supervisory styles, and specific training programs. Since selection is a critical step in developing organizational leaders, we begin with recruiting.

Selecting people for creativity, vision, and unconventionality is no easy task. Who, for that matter, knows what to look for? Indeed, corporate recruiters may actually go out of their way to avoid such characters: "To go after the occasional interesting oddball, the out-of-step type, is risky for recruiters' own careers. It's dangerous to be blamed for hiring weirdos, loners, and nerds, and that's the way some managers will see such unusual recruits. People like that will be irritants, disturbers of the peace. Besides, if they are hired but not supported by appropriate backup, they'll soon go away" (Leavitt, 1986, p. 158).

So we have a dilemma. While we may think we want more unconventional types, we may really not. But suppose your organization has had a change of heart and decides to take the risk and hire a few people who are imaginative and visionary. What would you look for? Most of the criteria we currently use in selection involve straightforward analytical skills. If you want to find people who by nature and experience are more likely to be pathfinding creative types, you will have to develop new criteria. You might begin by searching for individuals with stronger-than-average conceptual and creativity skills. In interviews, you might ask candidates to solve hypothetical case studies of strategic dilemmas or other problems requiring creative solutions. Moreover, there are tests and questionnaires to measure one's creativity (Kirton, 1976) as well as one's ability to think and plan over long time spans (Jacques, 1982, 1986). Certain needs might be tested, as well. For example, it appears that individuals who have strong power needs (McClelland, 1985) are likely to become more successful and possibly more effective leaders (House, 1988; Miner, 1978). Such measures could be used in your initial selection procedures.

Organizations might also try to ascertain whether candidates have a sense of determination and a passionate interest in their product or service. A degree of prior experience in their industry (especially diverse experience) might help, since creativity is enhanced by a depth and breadth of knowledge and experience. Candidates with a strong intrinsic motivation for their work may ultimately have the most potential to become visionaries. Yet in recruiting only limited attention is directed to intrinsic motivation. Interview questions focusing on the candidate's favorite tasks and projects in the past may be revealing in this respect. As well, once recruited, junior managers should be matched to tasks that stimulate their intrinsic motivation as this appears to enhance their ability to be innovative (Amabile and Gryskiewicz, 1987).

Job experiences may be particularly vital to enhancing the development of visionary leaders. Surely one reason why we have more tactical managers than visionary leaders is because of excessive functional specialization. When executives are promoted through the ranks of a single function, it is hard for them to lead from a generalist's perspective. Remember John DeLorean's early experiences at Packard where he was involved in the many facets of a car's development? This is the type of experience that may often be required (preferably during the early stages of one's career). Moreover, there should be far greater exposure to *all* the dimensions of a particular function. So, for example, manufacturing trainees should have experience in most areas of their company's production process. In either case, such experiences should include job rotation with considerable line and field experience, which may heighten sensitivity to one's markets and to the organization's character. As a person's experience widens, so does his ability to perceive the breadth of issues needed to understand his operation strategically. Such experiences should involve considerable opportunities to experiment with leadership.

I cannot emphasize this factor enough. Research shows that challenging assignments are the most helpful experience for developing executive talent. Jack Welch, the widely praised chairman of General Electric, started his career at GE with profit-and-loss responsibility (at age 27) for a new and untried plastic material called Lexan. At the time, there were no markets for the product and few sales. It was a difficult assignment for a rookie manager. Unconstrained by tradition or bureaucracy, however, he experimented with unconventional approaches to making the business successful. He formed joint ventures with Japan and the Netherlands before such alliances became popular, and he positioned Lexan as a replacement for glass. His tactics soon showed surprising results, and Lexan became a commercial success. Experiences such as this can give young managers an opportunity to experiment with their leadership style as well as learn the business.

Decentralization is especially critical to this process. Companies skilled at creating leaders push responsibility downward and, in turn, create more challenging jobs. Many of these companies create as many small units as possible or else develop challenging opportunities by emphasizing growth through new products and new ventures or by using temporary and frequently restructured teams and task forces. In this way chances are increased that managers will develop a broad conception of their organization's role and have greater opportunities to lead.

Supervisory style may also play a role in the creative abilities associated with visioning. In R&D laboratories, for instance, a high measure of individual autonomy is critical for creativity. While the project manager retains "strategic autonomy" for a project's overall direction, he or she allows "operational autonomy" regarding the means by which the overall goal will be achieved. In one study of especially creative R&D groups, it was found that "the best managers are those who ask questions. The role of the manager is to make clear what the objective, directions, and purpose are, to set up a picture or long-term objective that a person will be working toward. Once the operation is under way, the managers should then provide an environment where a lot of questions are asked. He should be non-judgemental—the people working on the project, or their peers, should make the judgements" (Amabile and Gryskiewicz, 1987, p. 27). These management practices helped to promote creative approaches to problems. Marketing managers or manufacturing managers could adopt a similar process—setting overall objectives but leaving the creative business of getting to those objectives up to subordinates.

Training visioning skills, however, is a more difficult task. In the first place, some of us have certain "cognitive personalities" or backgrounds that lend themselves to imagination and creativity, but others of us do not. Moreover, vision is a much more complex and personal experience than a workshop could ever hope to capture and then train. Our focus, then, should begin with the basic skills of creativity and problem solving. Techniques such as "synectics" (Gordon, 1961) and "Janusian thinking" (Rothenburg, 1979) may aid managers in developing such skills. There are, as well, programs offered by organizations such as the Center for Creative Leadership (Greensboro, North Carolina) that focus specifically on helping managers to develop their creative abilities and on helping corporations to identify aspects of the corporate environment that inhibit creativity. Sessions such as the Quick Environment Scanning Technique (QUEST) may be useful in stimulating vision. In such programs, managers come together to brainstorm about future opportunities and threats in the marketplace and to determine the implications for their organization's strategy. The brainstorming nature of these sessions forces managers to explore strategic and tactical options that the conventions of their organizations would normally preclude.

But training in creativity will take root only if organizations support the experimentation it takes to unlearn less creative approaches. For the fastest way to kill incipient creativity skills is to place them in an organization that demands uncreative ways of thinking and has few rewards for initiative. As well, learning creativity demands individual effort supported by certain organizational factors. Stanford psychologist Harold Leavitt (1986) argues that the teaching methods most helpful for creative problem solving are enabling methods like relaxation. Essentially they involve turning off the "rules of reason" we rely on every day. Organizations can encourage this dynamic in several ways. They can promote "planned playfulness"— a day of unconventional activities, say, or a retreat to an unusual site. Rewards, especially intrinsic rewards, can be powerful stimulants. Extrinsic rewards, however, are dangerous because they can drive out intrinsic motivation. If I'm *paid* to do something, it may lose some of its appeal. And sometimes bonuses for creative achievements can backfire for social reasons—for example, one person may get a bonus for an achievement that others feel they also contributed to.

But the most important thing organizations can do is *approve* of creativity. Social disapproval, Leavitt (1986) argues, is the most powerful killer of creativity, for social fears block the expression of ideas. Companies should instead provide support for innovative champions and back them against opponents. They should also avoid punishing certain types of innovative failure. Efforts based on quality, perseverance, and energy, for instance, should not be penalized.

Communication Skills. As we saw in Chapter Four, communication skills are vitally important for business leaders. Yet they are among the most overlooked of the leadership skills. Most managers simply need a basic course in speaking skills such as those offered by Dale Carnegie. Beyond such programs, however, senior executives might find it useful to take training in persuasion and rhetoric. As well, we have seen that simply by adding more stories and metaphors and employing paralanguage, business leaders can often give their messages greater impact. Every basic program must address at least the following dimensions (Kruger, 1970, pp. 4-5):

- Improvement of vocal expressiveness—to develop skills in the rate, pitch, and loudness of one's voice
- Learning to articulate clearly—to eliminate poor speaking habits and to enhance the way one articulates

- Improvement of body language—to relate the body's expressions to the message one is delivering so that the eyes, hands, and face are all coordinated while speaking
- Learning to develop, organize, and support ideas—to present one's ideas and facts clearly and persuasively without a lot of clutter

The written word and the spoken word must be presented differently from each other if they are to have an impact. Far too many managers and executives treat these two modes of expression as the same. Yet research has found significant differences between effective writing and effective speech. The spoken word, for example, in contrast to the written word, tends to have shorter phrases and words, more interruptions and parenthetical remarks, simpler, loosely constructed sentences, more personal pronouns ("we," "you," and "I"), greater informality, more restatements and summaries, more frequent use of dialogue, more examples, imagery, and illustrations, and an emphasis on the concrete rather than the abstract (Kruger, 1970, p. 341).

Managers can use various rhetorical devices—such as repeating a phrase or word—to emphasize key points. When Lincoln concluded the Gettysburg Address, he exclaimed "government of the people, by the people, for the people"—not "government of, by, and for the people," which would have lacked the emphasis on "people" that Lincoln wanted to convey. Rhetorical questions, as well, can be used to stimulate and direct attention. Metaphors should be used to clarify the abstract, to express certain feelings, or to make a point more vividly. Martin Luther King, Jr., constantly used metaphors to express powerful feelings: "With this faith we will be able to hew out of the mountain of despair a stone of hope. With this faith we will be able to transform the jangling discords of our nation into a beautiful symphony of brotherhood" (Kruger, 1979, p. 344). All these techniques can be learned. If you view film clips of the young Martin Luther King, you will see a fairly uninspiring speaker. As he refines his technique, however, he becomes one of the great speakers of the modern world.

Trust-Building Skills. Every leadership effort must be based on a foundation of trust between subordinates and the leader. Though much of this trust stems from the leader's own expertise and successes, some aspects might be trained. We could, for example, teach managers ways in which to be more expressive of their commitment to a project. Or they could be trained in impression management techniques to demonstrate self-confidence or shared values with subordinates. They could be trained, as well, in sensitivity skills to help them understand the needs and values of their subordinates. Experiences such as the group workshops offered by the National Training Laboratories might be helpful. Training could also emphasize the use of exemplary behavior involving personal sacrifice or provide opportunities to devise unconventional approaches to problems.

But personal commitment and a willingness to make sacrifices for a project must ultimately come from a sincere belief in what one is undertaking. Truly personal beliefs will lead to natural expressions of commitment that are more credible than the product of training seminars. Thus managers should be assigned to tasks that, whenever possible, hold a high degree of intrinsic motivation for them. As a result, they will tend to become naturally committed to the project's outcome. Organizations can promote this behavior by having senior managers consistently model exceptional personal commitment to their goals and projects. Since unconventionality is another element of the charismatic's trust-building process, organizations will have to become more tolerant of unique approaches by their managers. They will need to support such actions even though unconventionality, by definition, goes against the cultural grain of the organization.

Empowerment Skills. Of the various leadership practices associated with empowerment, some, such as the expression of confidence, are a matter of practice. Others, such as the staging of dramatic events, are more difficult to implement. Training could teach the practices themselves and the basic ideas behind the empowerment process as well as provide opportunities to experiment with them. It is critical, however, that training also emphasize the importance of fitting each practice to a manager's own context. In Chapter Six, for example, the leaders responded with practices that subordinates could relate to or that fit their character and needs—for instance, the squirtgun battles or the television set with a price placard. Certain situations, however, may not warrant empowerment. In some cases, subordinates may be unwilling to accept high expectations or assume greater responsibility. When staging playful, unconventional events, the manager's situation must be carefully considered. What signals do these events send to others in the organization? Could they inadvertently harm the manager's credibility, for instance? Like bestowing rewards and expressing confidence, these events can be used to excess and lose their meaning. Managers would have to be alerted—through workshops, for example—to the complexity behind "straightforward" practices.

Organizations themselves should encourage the use of empowerment practices by adopting them as management tools. They can emphasize reward systems that foster innovative performance. They can structure jobs that provide considerable autonomy and challenge. These practices encourage the development of empowered managers who themselves may become leaders who empower.

Each of these skills—visioning, communication, trust building, and empowerment—must be seen as complementary and training should therefore emphasize their integration. A typical program might involve three specific steps. The first step would focus on providing information on each skill area with feedback instruments to determine each participant's level of a particular skill. The second step would involve role playing and experimentation with the various skills. The final step might use a simulated management game designed to integrate the individual skills. To ensure that these skills are effectively transplanted, organizations would have to devise their selection procedures, rewards, jobs, supervision, and structures to support leadership behavior—a far more difficult task.

With some understanding of the training and development of charismatic leaders, let us shift our focus to a different set of issues. Assume for the moment that we are the senior management of an organization that employs or is considering employing an individual described as a charismatic leader. How do we manage these personalities effectively?

Managing the Charismatic Leader

How do we manage these unconventional leaders? For instance, how should senior managers supervise the activities of a charismatic division president given what we know about the charismatic's impulsive character and often countercultural behavior?

First of all, company executives and board members must recognize that these figures do have the potential to be disruptive and challenge the status quo. There are no sacred cows for the charismatic. This fact must be accepted before such leaders are brought into the organization. Management must carefully weigh the trade-offs between such challenges to the system and the organization's need for a significant transformation. Certainly senior management could attempt to obtain information on the leader's history of managing to determine how confrontive his behavior actually is and how he expresses his challenging actions. By doing this, management may be able to weigh the extent to which the charismatic will be effective given the organization's culture. This recommendation, however, may not always be so easy to implement.

In day-to-day managing, charismatics prefer extensive autonomy. From a supervisory viewpoint, however, autonomy should be balanced by clear objectives that have been mutually agreed upon. This strategy allows the organization to monitor and measure the charismatic's performance while permitting a measure of autonomy. Management might also wish to encourage the charismatic to surround himself with subordinates who are especially skilled at operational details and have strong connections to other areas of the company. Some charismatic leaders need to be complemented by others with strong operational skills.

Organizations should recognize, too, that a leader who is charismatic in one situation may not be so in another. The relational aspects of charismatic leadership are so critical that it may be wrong to select a leader assuming he will be charismatic in a new situation. It is a much more complicated process.

Let us speculate, then, where these leaders might be most appropriate. Say that you and I as senior management have found someone who has many of the charismatic qualities we have been describing. Remembering, of course, that a leader needs many more skills besides charisma to be effective, we believe this person could become a charismatic leader within our organization—but where?

First let us turn to a crisis situation. In crisis, people experience a loss of control, feelings of helplessness, and fears about their future. The organization's traditional ways of coping with problems no longer work, so people are susceptible to a leader who symbolizes rescue from this distress. In such cases, followers are more willing to submit to a strong individual— enter the charismatic leader with his clear vision and strength of conviction. We saw this process clearly at Chrysler Corporation when Lee Iacocca assumed command. Labor and management were willing to relinquish their demands and control for the security that Iacocca's leadership seemed to offer. So an operation in crisis might be an appropriate situation for a charismatic leader. Sometimes a potential crisis on the horizon leads senior management to search outside their ranks for a change agent. This was certainly the case with Arch McGill at AT&T. As well, in acquiring Electronic Data Systems (EDS) from its founder, Ross Perot, General Motors attempted indirectly to do much the same thing. By retaining the charismatic Perot and making him a member of the board of directors and the company's largest shareholder, a catalytic role was envisioned for him. Commenting on GM chairman Roger Smith's decision to buy EDS, *Business Week* said: "When Smith bought EDS's computer expertise, he knew he was also buying Perot's competitive spirit" (Mason, Mitchell, Hampton, and Frons, 1986, p. 62).

In both cases, Perot's and McGill's companies were experiencing or anticipating significant change. Perot and McGill were selected because they understood an industry or technology that the organization deemed important to its future and because they brought with them a fresh way of doing things. In both cases, senior management could initially tolerate the strong personalities of these men because they had something the organization needed. As McGill himself said, "An outsider brings a different perspective that is sometimes needed to push a company to ask critical questions that it might not otherwise have asked. I do many things from a different point of view. . . . I've spent most of my career in highly competitive businesses. The experience often suggests to me a new dimension on a problem, its magnitude, its importance, its potential contribution, and its risk" (Wilbins, 1982, p. 15). Their organizations were willing to accept an atypical personality in the hopes that change would follow. Of course, they did not anticipate that these leaders would prove far too unconventional and confrontive for them. Perot would publicly state: "Revitalizing GM is like teaching an elephant to tap dance. You find the sensitive spots and start poking." Two years later, in 1986, GM would buy out Perot's stockholdings for $700 million to end the poking.

Other environments may also be suitable for charismatic leaders. Recalling the earlier examples of charismatic entrepreneurs such as Steven Jobs and Donald Burr, we find some are drawn to entrepreneurial situations. If we think about the nature of entrepreneurial environments, we can see why they would attract charismatics. There are opportunities for monumental responsibility. Moreover, the environment's disorder and uncertainty make people susceptible to the charismatic's clear sense of vision. There is a high degree of risk; there is a great element of adventure; and there are no bureaucratic constraints. As well, the organization is a vehicle for realizing *their* dreams and no one else's.

Contrast this with organizations in a mature and stable industry. These are usually marked by bureaucratic controls, little personal autonomy, and limited room for innovation—a far less attractive environment for individuals with the skills and temperament of a charismatic leader. As well, an organization operating in a stable marketplace may not require such dominant and directive leadership. Stable and mature organizations are more likely to be averse to risk and to have routinized their operations to the point where rules and standard procedures, rather than leadership, are the primary means of managing. Instead, entrepreneurial ventures in organizations undergoing dramatic change or pressures for change may be the most appropriate situations for charismatic leaders.

Lessons for the Charismatic Leader

Let us say that you are a charismatic leader. What are the implications of this book for you? Above all you must be aware of the potential harm your actions may have—especially if you are operating in one unit of a huge organization. You must work to keep your superiors informed, and you must build political alliances with other powerful figures. Your greatest danger is that you will alienate the power blocs in your organization. As well, you must surround yourself with advisers who will challenge your views, and you must be willing to consider their ideas. Your enthusiasm for your ideas is a great strength in that it represents your sense of committing yourself fully and reflects on your creative spirit. The danger is that you may become so caught up in your ideas that you fail to consider contrary opinions or facts. You must learn to rein your enthusiasm in for a moment and cooly consider information that might challenge your mission. Finally, you have a great power in your hands—the dependence and commitment of your subordinates. Recognize that while their dependence heightens your own sense of importance, it also presents a potential liability for you both. Since part of your sense of power is derived from this relationship, do not encourage further dependence in order to heighten your own self-esteem. Recognize that you can easily become deluded by others' admiration and do things you might later regret. The moral is simply that you too are human.

Lessons for Organizations

What lessons can we draw for top management of the mature organization contemplating change or faced with managing a charismatic leader? For you, change is an unsettling process. You may sense that some changes are needed, that certain ways of approaching your markets or managing your people are outmoded. You may even flirt with change. But you also fear the leap into the unknown that wholesale change could bring. Thus you are often at the water's edge with one toe in. The charismatic leader offers the hope of taking you from the shoreline into the sea of change. Charismatics have the ideas and energy you need to rekindle your organization. They are exciting to listen to, and you are impressed by stories of their abilities to motivate and inspire a work force beyond expectations. But you wonder if you could not achieve the same end with a slightly more traditional leader, maybe someone from within. Few in your organization, however, may be capable of challenging your company's traditions and perspectives on the marketplace the way an outsider with vision could.

If you already have a charismatic leader, then you *know* there are dilemmas. These leaders are constantly challenging how things are done. They are impatient. They demand great autonomy. You worry about the opposition that sometimes grows up against them. Sometimes you are not sure how far you can trust their ideas. And you ask yourself where do we draw the line on support to their projects—especially if the projects appear to be failing? These are just a few of the dilemmas you face.

Prepare your organization, especially the charismatic's peers and superiors. Be direct in your comments to the charismatic leader if his actions are causing harm. Force yourself to be candid. Give in to him at times, and be careful not to pick fights over trivial issues. He may need these victories for his ego. This way he will be less disgruntled about the internal organization and more focused on the marketplace. Give him the latitude he needs for operational issues but hold him to mutually agreed goals and deadlines. Demand that he inform you early on of problems arising in his organization or with his goals. And do not allow his disgruntled peers to harbor negative feelings—force them to be open and constructive. Charismatics, as we have seen, demand special attention. You may ask yourself whether they are worth the attention and sometimes the headache. But just remember that change sometimes requires a jolt.

Conclusion

Effective leadership is one of the most powerful competitive advantages an organization can possess today. Sadly, it is one of the most underdeveloped and underutilized resources in many corporations and government agencies. Equally worrisome is the fact that it takes years, if not decades, to develop effective leadership in an organization.

If our industries are to remain competitive, we must quickly learn from the talents of our most exemplary leaders. Few leaders can teach us as much as charismatic leaders. Their skills in projecting a vision, in communicating, in building trust and commitment, and in empowering are unique. As the chapters in this book attest, they are masters of leading. They are also an integral part of our cultural heritage of entrepreneurship and individual expression.

In recent years, an emphasis on teamwork and participation has weakened this concept of personal leadership. The fascination with Japanese management practices has led to the replacement of the charismatic leader with the consensus-seeking leader. But we have swung perhaps too far on the pendulum. It is time to recognize the role that personal leadership must and has always played in organizational renewal and birth, especially in the West. The challenge for the 1990s will be to integrate these two opposing approaches to managing and to design organizations that can effectively combine the complementary perspectives. As Stanford psychologist Leavitt (1986) argues, the task will be to encourage both "the dedicated champion and the dedicated team worker, even trying to encourage both to reside within the same body" (p. 43). It is a daunting task but one that will, perhaps, define a new era of managing and leading in our organizations.

Resource

STUDYING CHARISMATIC AND NONCHARISMATIC LEADERS

This appendix reports my research design and methodology for the 1985 study of charismatic and noncharismatic business leaders. Here I will elaborate on the choices made in the research design and describe the sample selection procedures, the characteristics of the sample, and the research methods. The study was guided by two general questions:

- Can attributions about the personal behavior and management practices of charismatic leaders in business be distinguished from those made about noncharismatic leaders in business?
- Are there perceived behavioral differences in the influence process under charismatic leadership in business as compared to noncharismatic leadership in business?

To answer these questions, I designed the research project to compare four executives who had been described on an "a priori" basis as charismatic and effective leaders with four executives who had been described on an "a priori" basis as nonchar-

ismatic and effective. To avoid confounding leadership effectiveness with charisma, I examined only effective business leaders.
Exhibit 1 lists the study participants and their backgrounds. A

Exhibit 1. Background Data of Executive Sample.

1. Andrew Tobin*
    President
    Telcorp
    (Telephone Utility)
    $4.5 Billion Revenues

2. Douglas Lind*
    CEO
    Information Dynamics Corporation
    (Data Processing Firm)
    230 Employees
    $19 Million Revenues

3. Thomas Seeley*
    Executive Vice-President of Manufacturing
    Argo Computer
    (Computer Manufacturer)
    6,500 Employees (Mfg.)
    $3 Billion Revenues

4. Robert Lipp
    President of Chemical Bank and
    Executive Vice-President of Retail Banking Operations
    Chemical Bank
    3,750 Employees (Retail)
    $2.65 Billion in Assets (Retail)

5. Arch McGill
    President of Advanced Information Systems
    AT&T
    18,000 Employees
    $6 Billion Estimated Revenues

6. David Estes*
    CEO
    Software Research Corporation
    (Management Information Systems)
    325 Employees
    $25 Million Revenues

Exhibit 1. Background Data of Executive Sample, Cont'd.

---

7. Stephen Nash*
    President
    U.S. Brands
    (Packaged Food Company)
    3,500 Employees
    $200 Million Revenues

8. Mike Graham*
    President of Brewery Division
    Western Diversified Corporation
    (Beverage and Packaged Food Company)
    8,000 Employees
    $675 Million Revenues

---

*The names of these executives and their organizations have been disguised. Employee and sales figures are also disguised though approximate. The industry contexts, however, are the same or closely approximate.

field study with three types of data collection—interviews with executives, interviews with subordinates, and observation—was used to examine the research questions.

Selecting the Sample

For the initial selection of candidates, I relied on the outside perceptions of a panel consisting of senior faculty at the Harvard Business School and industry consultants who were well acquainted with the executives and their companies. The panel was comprised of twelve faculty members and four industry consultants. Each was asked to draw up two lists: one of highly effective, charismatic business leaders and another of highly effective, noncharismatic business leaders. A total of forty-eight candidates were suggested. Of these, fifteen were described as charismatic and thirty-three as noncharismatic. Several candidates appeared on more than one rater's list—but always under the same qualification as either charismatic or noncharismatic.

From these lists, candidates in each category were rank-ordered by frequency of mention. The four highest-ranking candidates from each category were then invited to participate in the study. In the charismatic category, those who received the highest number of recommendations ultimately became the study participants. In the noncharismatic category, several leaders received a greater number of recommendations but declined participation. Once in the field, interviews with subordinates were used for confirmation of these a priori judgments of the leader's charisma or lack of it.

The study intentionally did not employ an a priori operational definition of either charisma or charismatic leadership in the sample selection process but instead relied on outsiders' and subordinates' interpretations of the terms. This decision was based on the premise that charisma is an attributional phenomenon (Heider, 1958; Kelley, 1973). Since the study's aim was to explore the perceptions of subordinates with regard to charisma and its related attributes, it would have been improper to have imposed on them a set of distinguishing traits. The use of an operational definition would have implied such an imposition.

Drawing from Selznick (1957) and Katz and Kahn (1978), two leadership categories were used as criteria in the initial screening of candidates by the panel of raters. These categories were the leader's demonstrated responsibility for the definition of the organization's mission and role and for the institutional embodiment of purpose. Specifically, sample participants had to have been responsible for formulating, in large part, the goals and overall direction of their organizations. As well, they had to have been successful in implementing these goals into a level of organizational action that demonstrated exceptional achievement. This second factor, I felt, was most important, for as Selznick (1957, p. 63) argues: "The task of leadership is not only to make policy but to build it into the organization's social structure. This . . . is a creative task. It means shaping the 'character' of the organization, sensitizing it to ways of thinking and responding, so that increased reliability in the execution and elaboration of policy will be achieved according to its spirit as well as its letter." As judged by the experts on the panel, all the sample leaders met these criteria by demonstrating an ability to effect significant structural and social change within their organizations. All of the participants, for example, were responsible either for creating (or expanding) young, highly successful firms or for revitalizing mature organizations. Moreover, all managed highly profitable organizations relative to their industries.

The second selection criterion was the presence or absence of charisma. The use of a comparison group of noncharismatic leaders seemed imperative. As Campbell and Stanley (1963) argue: "Basic to scientific evidence . . . is the process of comparison, of recording differences, or of contrast. Any appearance of absolute knowledge, or intrinsic knowledge about singular isolated objects, is found to be illusory under analysis" (1963, p. 6).

My attempt to control for other factors was constrained by problems of access and time. Gaining access to senior executives is a formidable task. Their time is limited and often they are reluctant to be probed by projective tests, personality inventories, or other psychological instruments. To obtain qualified research participants, I was forced, for example, to make tradeoffs in terms of holding certain variables constant across the sample—such as the executive's managerial responsibilities (functional, divisional, or corporate) and specific organizational and industry contexts.

Certain variables, however, were common to all eight of the study's participants: their positions (each had the title and role of either chief executive officer or executive vice-president); the success of their organizations (all the companies were profitable, among the largest in their fields, and leaders in their specific market segments); and their backgrounds (all eight leaders were experienced senior executives and all were college educated—two held doctorates and four held master's degrees).

The sample size of eight was largely a function of the exploratory nature of the study. Since the phenomenon is quite complex, I decided that a small but intense field study would be most appropriate to capture its depth and richness. Limiting the number to eight executives also allowed for intensive interviewing and observation, while at the same time ensuring a large enough sample for us to draw reasonable conclusions on which to base hypotheses. Thus the findings of this exploratory study are presented as hypotheses to be tested by eventual studies on a larger scale. Moreover, they can be used to support or challenge the speculative hypotheses of organizational theorists.

Research Methods

The principal research methods used in the study were semistructured interviews, structured and unstructured observation, and the study of company documents and printed material. Psychological instruments were considered, but the sensitivity of participants did not permit their use. There were eight categories of data collection:

- On the executive's personal and family background
- On the executive's personal style, behavior, and management practices
- On the executive's basic values and assumptions about human needs, management, and his personal and organizational mission
- On the executive's leadership and management styles (including his strategic vision and influence style)
- On the executive's strategy for managing change, transition, and company growth
- On subordinates' relationships with the executive
- On subordinates' notions of benefits and rewards of association with the leader and his mission
- On the business and organizational context

The relationship between specific collection methods and the area of data collection is shown in Table 1.

Given that the study was largely exploratory, the combination of methods seemed appropriate. Survey methods and highly structured interviews, for example, would not have been amenable to pursuing spontaneously interesting leads. Semistructured interviews allowed for more freedom and tended to create greater informality, which often resulted in better rapport and, in turn, greater disclosure of sensitive and less obvious information.

Problems can arise with interviews, of course, particularly

Table 1. Relationship of Research Methods to Data Content.

Data	Interview with Executive	Interviews with Others	Observation	Printed Material
Personal/family background	P	S		S
Descriptors/behavior	P	P	P	
Values/core assumptions	P	P	P	
Leadership/management style (influence)	P	P	P	S
Strategy	P	P		S
Subordinate relationships	P	P	P	S
Subordinate needs	P	P	S	
Context	P	P	S	P

Note: P = primary source; S = secondary source.

semistructured interviews. There are potential problems in the reporting of management practices or events used to support attributional material. Respondent bias and incomplete perceptions are always possible. To minimize these distortions, I relied on cross-checking respondents' accounts and on observation.

The interview format of the project followed the general patterns outlined in Exhibits 2 and 3. The interview subjects

Exhibit 2. Interview Guide for Subordinates.

The key executives' staff members were generally interviewed for two to five hours each. These are some of the typical questions they were asked:

1. What is your background with the company? How long have you known and worked with the executive?
2. Tell me about your relationship with the executive. How do other subordinates relate to him? Is there a good fit between subordinates and the executive? How so?
3. How would you describe the executive's management style and practices? What are some specific examples of his behavior? Do you consider him to be a leader? How would you describe his leadership style and character? His influence style?
4. (If subordinates spontaneously described the executive as a charismatic leader, they were usually asked the following questions.) What

(continued on next page)

Exhibit 2. Interview Guide for Subordinates, Cont'd.

do you mean by charismatic leader? What does he do that makes him a charismatic leader? What makes up his charisma? What, for you, are the attributes that comprise his charisma? (At the end of the interview, subordinates who had not described the executive as charismatic were typically asked the following question: Would you describe the executive as a charismatic leader? If the answer was yes, the same questions as above would be asked. If the answer was no, subordinates were asked why he was not perceived as charismatic. Most respondents cited behaviors of a charismatic leader they had known or were familiar with to describe their leader's lack of charisma.)

5. What is the leader's behavior like?
6. How about his basic values when it comes to managing people? His philosophy of life?
7. What do you know about the leader's family and personal background?
8. How is he perceived by others in the company?
9. Which of his qualities do you wish you had? Which of your needs does his leadership personally fulfill?
10. How does he compare in his leadership to others you have known?
11. Is he an effective motivator? How does he do it? How does he get others to do what he wants them to do?
12. How has he managed the changes in his organization? What was his specific strategy? Was it effective and why? How would you describe his image of the company's future? Is it effective?
13. Tell me about the organization. What is the company's history? What is the background of the people here? What is top management like? How do people relate to one another? Are there certain widely accepted types of behavior or certain kinds of behavior that are not accepted? What is the culture like? How would you describe the organization if it were a single individual? Tell me about the company's situation before the executive's arrival and afterward. Tell me about your industry and the competition—industry and company growth rates, competitive structure of the industry, product-driven or market-driven, maturity, environmental turbulence.

Exhibit 3. Interview Guide for Executives.

The executives were interviewed from two to six times. These are some of the typical questions they were asked:

1. Describe your job.
2. Describe your career history.
3. Describe the characteristics of your industry and your company's environment.

Exhibit 3. Interview Guide for Executives, Cont'd.

---

4. Describe your organization.
5. What was the situation in your company (or operating unit) before you assumed your present position?
6. What are the key things that have happened since you took this job? What did you do? Why? What effect did your actions have? What problems did you encounter and how did you handle them?
7. How would you describe your management style and management practices? How do you behave specifically? How would others describe your behavior? Has it changed over the years? How?
8. How do you see your role as a leader? How would others see it? Has it changed over the years? How?
9. How would you describe your personality? How would others describe it?
10. What are your basic beliefs about people and life?
11. What is your vision for this company (or division)? How did it come about?
12. How do you motivate and influence your subordinates? In other words, how do you get them to do what you want them to do? What are some recent examples?
13. What have been the key factors to your success?
14. What were your childhood and family background like?
15. What are your personal interests?
16. (For events observed during the day, the following questions typically were asked.) What exactly were you trying to do when you ...? Why were you trying to do this? Why did you do it in that way? How typical were the events I observed?

---

were the executives and their subordinates. An average of eight subordinates were interviewed at each site. (At one site, however, I initially gained access to only three, though an additional three participated one year later.) Subordinates represented a mix of managers one to three levels below the leader. In the original design, approximately fifty-six hours of interview time were spent with the eight executives (six to eight hours with each), and approximately one hundred eighty hours were spent interviewing a total of sixty-four subordinates (two to four hours with each). On average, two hundred pages of interview data were collected at each site. A year later, in 1986, I returned to several sites and spent an additional twenty-five hours with executives and forty hours with subordinates including interviews with an additional ten subordinates.

The second research method, observation, while more

time consuming, provided firsthand and more thorough coverage of the leader's behavior and allowed for validation of the attributional data. In all, I spent approximately one hundred twenty-eight hours in observation (sixteen hours with each executive) and an additional sixty-four hours a year later. Observation provided the opportunity to witness relationships in action and to link and test statements from interviews with actual events. As well, it proved useful in detecting habitual or culturally determined activities that participants only vaguely perceived.

There are, of course, questions of validity with data collected through observation—for example, I had no control over the sequencing and timing of events. Thus I may have missed important events that occurred only rarely, or I may have witnessed rare events and misinterpreted them as commonplace. I was careful, however, to ask respondents whether the events I had seen were commonplace or rare. The eight research subjects, as well as their subordinates, commented on the representativeness of the observational periods. There is also the question of reactive effects caused by my presence—for example, the leaders may have been on their best behavior while I was observing them. Though it is impossible to measure such effects, I felt that my presence in meetings and interviews had a noticeable effect only for the first five or ten minutes. Leaders and their subordinates then became far less aware of my presence and more engrossed in their discussion or activities.

The third research method, the study of company documents and printed material, helped to provide historical information on the executive and his company's background. Generally this material included company brochures, annual reports, financial and strategic documents, published articles on the company and the executive, résumés, organizational charts, and key memos and reports.

In summary, then, research data comparing the charismatic versus noncharismatic leaders were collected along the following dimensions:

- Executives' self-descriptions of their behavior, management practices, personal traits, and styles of influence

- Subordinates' descriptions of their leader
- My observations of the leader
- Published descriptions of the leader

Each source was used to cross-validate the other. In all cases, the executives were interviewed first. Afterward a period of observation was conducted at five sites and then subordinate interviews (or, in the case of Graham, Seeley, and Tobin, subordinate interviews and then observation).

Categorizing Leaders as Charismatic

Ultimately, on the basis of subordinates' perceptions, the sample of charismatic versus noncharismatic leaders assumed a scalar quality. Employing a coding system based on the percentage of subordinates who described their leader as charismatic, I found that three leaders emerged with high percentages of subordinates describing them as charismatic (McGill, Seeley, and Lipp), three had moderate to low percentages (Tobin, Estes, and Lind), and two (Nash and Graham) were described as not at all charismatic in their leadership (see Table 2). This categorization matched the suggestions of the expert panel on all but Lind and Tobin. The protocol to determine these categories consisted of coding a subordinate's description of a leader in the following response criteria: (1) The subordinate spontaneously used the terms *charisma* or *charismatic leader* in his or her description of the leader; or (2) the subordinate described the leader as being charismatic or noncharismatic when asked a direct question at the end of the interview.

The interview protocol was designed to make these response categories possible by using the following procedure. In interviews, I would wait for respondents to describe spontaneously their leader as charismatic, rather than risk the introduction of bias by asking the question myself. I asked the direct question only at the very end of an interview and only if a respondent had not spontaneously described the leader as charismatic during the interview. In the interviews, there was also a range of subjective descriptions concerning the strength of the

Table 2. Ranking of Executives by Subordinates' Perceptions
of Their Charisma.

Executive	Total Interviewees[a]	Column A[b]	Column B[c]	Column C[d]
McGill	12	11 (92%)	1 (8%)	12 (100%)
Seeley	12	11 (92%)	1 (8%)	12 (100%)
Lipp	6	6 (100%)	0 (0%)	6 (100%)
Tobin	10	4 (40%)	2 (20%)	6 (60%)
Estes	8	3 (38%)	1 (12%)	4 (50%)
Lind	10	2 (20%)	0 (0%)	2 (20%)
Nash	8	0	0	0
Graham	8	0	0	0

[a]1985 study plus 1986 follow-up study.
[b]Number of respondents who spontaneously described their leader as charismatic for themselves and/or others in the organization.
[c]Number of respondents who did not spontaneously describe their leader as charismatic but who responded at the end of the interview to the question "Would you consider your leader charismatic?" with a yes.
[d]Total number of respondents who either spontaneously or after direct questioning described their leader as charismatic for themselves or others in the organization.

leader's charisma; these descriptions, however, were not weighted in the coding system due to their irregular use.

The Process of Inquiry

After identifying an executive as a possible candidate for the study, I telephoned him directly to invite his participation, explaining the study and the extent of his involvement. The study was described as focusing on leadership and management style. At no point, before or during the inquiry, were the words *charisma* or *charismatic leadership* used to describe the study, either to the executives or to subordinates. I would simply state that the study was to understand the executive's "management style." If he agreed to participate, an initial meeting was held to discuss the details and logistics of the study. At the same time, I asked for written information on the executive and his company; this usually consisted of a résumé, an organizational chart, product brochures, business plans, and articles on the industry, company, and executive. I then conducted a preliminary interview on the executive's career history and management style.

Approximately one month later, a second visit was arranged. At this time, I interviewed the executive for several hours and then spent two to three days observing the executive in action. Afterward I interviewed key subordinates. At three sites, however, subordinates' interviews preceded observation. Observation proved the most difficult methodology when it came to securing the participants' approval. Several were involved in highly competitive situations and were concerned about information leakage. Others traveled extensively and were not available except on rare occasions. Even in the worst case, however, I was able to observe the equivalent of at least two full days of the executive's behavior in meetings (three executives); in the best case, I spent a minimum of three full days with the executive (five executives).

After the final visit, all my information was organized and analyzed by case. Using content analysis, I coded raw data into specific attribute and behavioral categories so that descriptive material could be compared across the sample based on subordinates' perceptions, leaders' self-descriptions, and my observations. I based the categories on descriptors used by interviewees or discerned during observation. These were either employed "as is" (wherever identical labels could be found across the sample) or to construct broader categories (where labels of a similar nature were used). Enumeration was based on the appearance of a label in interviews or during observation. From these data came the final analysis for the study. Approximately one year later (1986), I returned to interview the executives and subordinates for additional information and often to conduct further observation.

REFERENCES

Altemeyer, R. "Education in the Arts and Sciences: Divergent Paths." Unpublished doctoral dissertation, Carnegie Institute of Technology, 1966.

Amabile, T. M., and Gryskiewicz, S. S. "Creativity in the R&D Laboratory." Technical report no. 30. Greensboro, N.C.: Center for Creative Leadership, 1987.

Andrews, K. R. *The Concept of Corporate Strategy.* Homewood Ill.: Irwin, 1987.

"AT&T's Supersalesman Hangs It Up." *Business Week,* June 20, 1983, pp. 32–34.

"AT&T Unit's McGill Resigns, Duties Split Between Two Officials." *Wall Street Journal,* June 8, 1983, p. 26.

Avolio, B. J., and Bass, B. M. "Transformational Leadership, Charisma and Beyond." Working paper. Binghamton: School of Management, State University of New York, 1985.

Avolio, B. J., and Bass, B. M. "Charisma and Beyond." In J. G. Hunt, B. R. Baliga, H. P. Dachler, and C. A. Schriesheim (eds.), *Emerging Leadership Vistas.* Boston: Lexington, 1987.

Bandura, A. "Self-Efficacy: Toward a Unifying Theory of Behavioral Change." *Psychological Review,* 1977, *84* (2), 191–215.

Bandura, A. *Social Foundations of Thought and Action: A Social-Cognitive View.* Englewood, N.J.: Prentice-Hall, 1986.

193

Bass, B. M. *Leadership and Performance Beyond Expectations.* New York: Free Press, 1985.

Beer, M. *Organizational Change and Development: A Systems View.* Santa Monica: Goodyear, 1980.

Bem, D. J. *Beliefs, Attitudes, and Human Affairs.* Belmont, Calif.: Brooks/Cole, 1970.

Bennis, W., and Nanus, B. *Leaders.* New York: Harper & Row, 1985.

Bennis, W. G., Berlew, D. E., Schein, E. H., and Steele, F. I. *Interpersonal Dynamics.* Homewood, Ill.: Dorsey Press, 1973.

Berlew, D. E. "Leadership and Organizational Excitement." *California Management Review,* Winter 1974, *17* (2), 21–30.

Bienkowski, J. "What Happens to Home Banking Now?" *Bankers Monthly,* June 1986, *103,* 10.

Block, P. *The Empowered Manager.* San Francisco: Jossey-Bass, 1987.

Borgida, E., and Nisbett, R. E. "The Differential Impact of Abstract vs. Concrete Information on Decisions." *Journal of Applied Psychology,* 1977, 7 (3), 258–271.

Bowers, J. W., and Osborn, M. M. "Attitudinal Effects of Selected Types of Concluding Metaphors in Persuasive Speeches." *Speech Monographs,* 1966, *33,* 147–155.

Bryne, D. *The Attraction Paradigm.* New York: Academic Press, 1977.

Bucher, L. *Accidental Millionaire.* New York: Paragon House, 1988.

Burke, K. *The Philosophy of Literary Form.* London: University of California Press, 1973.

Burns, J. M. *Roosevelt: The Lion and the Fox.* New York: Harcourt Brace Jovanovich, 1956.

Burns, J. M. *Leadership.* New York: Harper & Row, 1978.

Byrne, J. A. "Up, Up and Away?" *Business Week,* Nov. 25, 1985, pp. 80–94.

Calder, B. J. "An Attribution Theory of Leadership." In B. M. Staw and G. R. Salancik (eds.), *New Directions in Organizational Behavior.* Chicago: St. Clair, 1977.

Campbell, D. T., and Stanley, J. C. *Experimental and Quasi-Experimental Designs for Research.* Skokie, Ill.: Rand McNally, 1963.

Carlzon, J. *Moments of Truth.* Cambridge, Mass.: Ballinger, 1987.

Clark, B. R. "The Organizational Saga in Higher Education." *Administrative Science Quarterly,* 1972, *17,* 178–184.

Conger, J. A. "Charismatic Leadership in Business: An Exploratory Study." Unpublished doctoral dissertation, School of Business Administration, Harvard University, 1985.

Conger, J. A., and Kanungo, R. N. "Towards a Behavioral Theory of Charismatic Leadership in Organizational Settings." *Academy of Management Review,* 1987, *12* (4), 637–647.

Conger, J. A. "Theoretical Foundations of Charismatic Leadership." In J. A. Conger, R. N. Kanungo, and Associates (eds.), *Charismatic Leadership.* San Francisco: Jossey-Bass, 1988.

Conger, J. A., and Kanungo, R. N. "Behavioral Dimensions of Charismatic Leadership." In J. A. Conger, R. N. Kanungo, and Associates (eds.), *Charismatic Leadership.* San Francisco: Jossey-Bass, 1988a.

Conger, J. A., Kanungo, R. N., and Associates (eds.), *Charismatic Leadership: The Elusive Factors in Organizational Effectiveness.* San Francisco: Jossey-Bass, 1988b.

Conger, J. A., and Kanungo, R. N. "Charismatic Leadership in Organizations: Test of a Behavioral Model." Paper presented at meeting of Academy of Management, Anaheim, Calif., Aug. 1988c.

Conger, J. A., and Kanungo, R. N. "Conclusion: Patterns and Trends in Studying Charismatic Leadership." In J. A. Conger, R. N. Kanungo, and Associates (eds.), *Charismatic Leadership.* San Francisco: Jossey-Bass, 1988d.

Conger, J. A., and Kanungo, R. N. "The Empowerment Process: Integrating Theory and Practice." *Academy of Management Review,* 1988e, *13* (3), 471–482.

Conger, J. A., and Kanungo, R. N. "Training Charismatic Leadership: A Risky and Critical Task." In J. A. Conger, R. N. Kanungo, and Associates (eds.), *Charismatic Leadership.* San Francisco: Jossey-Bass, 1988f.

Daly, M. "The Real DeLorean Story." *New York,* Nov. 8, 1982, pp. 30–38.

Davies, J. C. "Charisma in the 1952 Campaign." *American Political Science Review,* 1954, *48,* 1083–1102.

Dougherty, J. S. *Visa International: The Management of Change.* Boston: Harvard Business School, 1981.

Dow, T. E., Jr. "The Theory of Charisma." *Sociological Quarterly,* 1969, *10,* 306–318.

Downton, J. V., Jr. *Rebel Leadership.* New York: Free Press, 1973.

Drucker, P. F. "Leadership: More Doing Than Dash." *Wall Street Journal,* Jan. 6, 1988.

Dreman, D. *Contrarian Investment Strategy.* New York: Random House, 1979.

Edelman, M. *The Symbolic Uses of Politics.* Urbana: Unversity of Illinois Press, 1964.

Eisenstadt, S. N. *Max Weber.* Chicago: University of Chicago Press, 1968.

Erickson, B., Lind, E. A., Johnson, B. C., and O'Barr, W. M. "Speech Style and Impression Formation in a Court Setting: The Effects of 'Powerful' and 'Powerless' Speech." *Journal of Experimental Social Psychology,* 1978, *14,* 266–279.

Erikson, E. *Identity, Youth, and Crisis.* New York: Norton, 1968.

Festinger, L. *A Theory of Cognitive Dissonance.* Evanston, Ill.: Row, Peterson, 1957.

Foust, D., and King, R. W. "Why Federal Express Has Overnight Anxiety." *Business Week,* Nov. 29, 1987, pp. 62–66.

Freemesser, G. F., and Kaplan, H. B. "Self-Attitudes and Deviant Behavior: The Case of the Charismatic Religious Movement." *Journal of Youth and Adolescence,* 1976, *5* (1), 1–9.

Freiberger, P., and Swaine, M. *Fire in the Valley.* Berkeley: Osborne/McGraw-Hill, 1984.

French, J. R., Jr., and Raven, B. H. "The Bases of Social Power." In D. Cartwright (ed.), *Studies in Social Power.* Ann Arbor: University of Michigan Press, 1959.

Galanter, M. "Charismatic Religious Sects and Psychiatry: An Overview." *American Journal of Psychiatry,* 1982, *139* (2), 1539–1548.

Garrett, E. M. "The Troops are Restless at People Express." *Venture,* 1986, *8,* 102–104.

Gay, V. "Archie McGill and His Ma." *Boston Globe,* May 2, 1982, p. A8.

Gordon, W.J.J. *Synectics: The Development of Creative Capacity*. New York: Collier, 1961.

Hannan, M. T., and Freeman, J. "Structural Inertia and Organizational Change." *American Sociological Review*, 1984, *49*, 149–164.

Heider, F. "Social Perception and Phenomenal Causality." *Psychological Review*, 1944, *51*, 358–374.

Heider, F. *The Psychology of Interpersonal Relations*. New York: Wiley, 1958.

Helmich, D. L. "Corporate Succession: An Examination." *Academy of Management Journal*, 1975, *18*, 429–441.

Helmich, D. L. "Leader Flows and Organizational Process." *Academy of Management Journal*, 1978, *21*, 463–478.

Helmich, D. L., and Brown, W. "Successor Type and Organizational Change in the Corporate Enterprise." *Administrative Science Quarterly*, 1972, *17*, 371–381.

Horton, R. B. "Inside the Managerial Psyche." *Darden Report*, Winter 1988, pp. 9–16.

House, R. J. "A 1976 Theory of Charismatic Leadership." In J. G. Hunt and L. L. Larson (eds.), *Leadership: The Cutting Edge*. Carbondale: Southern Illinois University Press, 1977.

House, R. J. "Exchange and Charismatic Theories of Leadership." In A. Kaiser, G. Reber, and W. Wundered (eds.), *Handwörterbuch der Führung*. Stuttgart: C. E. Poescel Verlag, 1985.

House, R. J. "Power and Personality in Complex Organizations." In L. L. Cummings and B. M. Staw (eds.), *Research in Organizational Behavior: An Annual Review of Critical Essays and Reviews*. Vol. 10. Greenwich, Conn.: JAI Press, 1988.

House, R., and Singh, J. "Organizational Behavior: Some New Directions for I/O Psychology." *Annual Review of Psychology*, 1987, *37*, 669–718.

House, R. J., Woycke, J., and Fodor, E. M. "Charismatic and Noncharismatic Leaders: Differences in Behavior and Effectiveness." In J. A. Conger, R. N. Kanungo, and Associates (eds.), *Charismatic Leadership*. San Francisco: Jossey-Bass, 1988.

Howell, J. M. "A Laboratory Study of Charismatic Leadership."

Paper presented at the annual meeting of Academy of Management, San Diego, 1985.

Iacocca, L. "Iacocca." *Fortune,* Aug. 29, 1988, pp. 38–43.

Iacocca, L., and Novak, W. *Iacocca: An Autobiography.* New York: Bantam Books, 1984.

Jacques, E. "The Development of Intellectual Capability: A Discussion of Stratified Systems Theory." *Journal of Applied Behavioral Science,* 1986, *22,* 361–383.

Jacques, E. *The Form of Time.* London: Heinemann, 1982.

James, R. D. "Visa Chief Practices What He Preaches in Attacking Rival American Express." *Wall Street Journal,* June 3, 1981, p. 16.

Janis, I. L. *Victims of Group Think.* Boston: Houghton Mifflin, 1972.

Jennings, E. J. *An Anatomy of Leadership.* New York: McGraw-Hill, 1960.

Kahn, J. P. "Steven Jobs of Apple Computer: The Missionary of Micros." *Inc.,* April 1984, p. 83.

Katz, D., and Kahn, R. L. *The Social Psychology of Organizations.* New York: Wiley, 1978.

Keller, J. J., and Wilson, J. W. "Why Zap Mail Finally Got Zapped." *Business Week,* Oct. 13, 1986, pp. 48–49.

Kelley, H. H. *Causal Schemata and the Attribution Process.* Morristown, N.J.: General Learning Press, 1972.

Kelley, H. H. "The Process of Causal Attribution." *American Psychologist,* 1973, *28,* 107–128.

Kelman, H. C. "Compliance, Identification, and Internalization: Three Processes of Attitude Change." *Journal of Conflict Resolution,* 1958, *2,* 51–60.

Kets de Vries, M.F.R. "Origins of Charisma: Ties That Bind the Leader and the Led." In J. A. Conger, R. N. Kanungo, and Associates (eds.), *Charismatic Leadership.* San Francisco: Jossey-Bass, 1988.

Kets de Vries, M.F.R., and Miller, D. *The Neurotic Organization.* San Francisco: Jossey-Bass, 1984.

Kiechel, W. "Corporate Strategy for the 1990's." *Fortune,* Feb. 29, 1988, pp. 34–42.

Kirton, M. "Adaptors and Innovators: A Description and Measure." *Journal of Applied Psychology,* 1976, *61* (5), 622–629.

Kleinke, C. L. *First Impressions: The Psychology of Encountering Others.* Englewood Cliffs, N.J.: Prentice-Hall, 1975.

Kotter, J. P. *The General Managers.* New York: Free Press, 1982.

Kotter, J. P. *The Leadership Factor.* New York: Free Press, 1988.

Kruger, A. N. *Effective Speaking.* New York: Van Nostrand Reinhold Co., 1970.

Lamb, R. B. *Running American Business.* New York: Basic Books, 1987.

Leavitt, H. J. *Corporate Pathfinders.* Homewood, Ill.: Dow Jones-Irwin, 1986.

Levin, H. *Grand Delusions.* New York: Viking Press, 1983.

Levinson, H., and Rosenthal, S. *CEO: Corporate Leadership in Action.* New York: Basic Books, 1984.

Lodahl, A. "Crises in Values and the Success of the Unification Church." Unpublished B.A. thesis, Cornell University, 1982.

McClelland, D. C. *Human Motivation.* Glenview, Ill: Scott Foresman, 1985.

Martin, J., and Powers, M. E. "Truth or Corporate Propaganda: The Value of a Good War Story." In L. R. Pondy, P. J. Frost, G. Morgan, and T. C. Dandridge (eds.), *Organizational Symbolism.* Greenwich, Conn.: JAI Press, 1983.

Martin, J., and Siehl, C. "Organizational Culture and Counterculture: An Uneasy Symbiosis." *Organizational Dynamics,* 1983, *12* (2), 52–64.

Maslow, A. H. *Motivation and Personality.* New York: Harper & Row, 1954.

Maslow, A. H. *Eupsychian Management.* Homewood, Ill.: Richard D. Irwin and Dorsey Press, 1965.

Maslow, A. H. *Towards a Psychology of Being.* (2nd ed.) Princeton: Van Nostrand Reinhold, 1968.

Mason, T., Mitchell, R., Hampton, W. J., and Frons, M. "Ross Perot's Crusade." *Business Week,* Oct. 6, 1986, pp. 60–65.

Merry, G. W. *Polaroid–Kodak.* Boston: Harvard Business School, 1976.

Miller, D., and Friesen, P. H. "Momentum and Revolution in Organizational Adaptation." *Academy of Management Journal,* 1980, *23,* 591–614.

Miller, D., and Friesen, P. H. *Organizations: A Quantum View.* Englewood Cliffs, N.J.: Prentice-Hall, 1984.

Miner, J. B. "Twenty Years of Research on Role-Motivation Theory of Managerial Effectiveness." *Personnel Psychology,* 1978, *31,* 739-760.

Mintzberg, H. *The Nature of Managerial Work.* New York: Harper & Row, 1973.

Mintzberg, H. "If You're Not Serving Bill and Barbara, Then You're Not Serving Leadership." In J. G. Hunt, U. Sekaran, and C. A. Schreisheim (eds.), *Leadership: Beyond Establishment Views.* Carbondale: Southern Illinois University Press, 1982.

Mintzberg, H., and Waters, J. A. "Of Strategies, Deliberate and Emergent." *Strategic Management Journal,* 1985, *6,* 257-272.

Morris, C. W. *Signs, Language and Behavior.* New York: Prentice-Hall, 1949.

Naisbitt, J. *Megatrends.* New York: Warner Books, 1984.

Nathan, J. *Entrepreneurs: Viewers Guide and Transcript.* Waltham, Mass.: Nathan Tyler, 1986.

Norman, J. R. "People Is Plunging, But Burr Is Staying Cool." *Business Week,* July 7, 1986, pp. 31-32.

Norman, J. R., and Byrne, J. A. "Nice Going, Frank, But Will It Fly?" *Business Week,* Sept. 29, 1986, pp. 34-35.

O'Reilly, B. "Steve Jobs Tries to Do It Again." *Fortune,* May 23, 1988, pp. 83-88.

Osborn, M. M., and Ehninger, D. "The Metaphor in Public Address." *Speech Monograph,* 1962, *29,* 228.

Oskamp, S. "The Relationship of Clinical Experience and Training Methods to Several Criteria of Clinical Prediction." *Psychological Monographs: General and Applied,* 1962, *76* (28), entire issue.

Perkins, D. N. *The Mind's Best Work.* Cambridge: Harvard University Press, 1981.

Pfeffer, J. *Power in Organizations.* Marshfield, Mass.: Pitman Publishing, 1981.

Pondy, L. "Leadership as a Language Game." In M. W. McCall, Jr., and M. M. Lombardo (eds.), *Leadership: Where Else Can We Go?* Durham: Duke University Press, 1978.

Quinn, J. B. *Strategies for Change: Logical Incrementalism.* Homewood, Ill.: Richard D. Irwin, 1980.

Reinganum, M. "The Effect of Executive Succession on Stockholder Wealth." *Administrative Science Quarterly,* 1985, *30,* 46–60.

Rhodes, L. "That Daring Young Man and His Flying Machine." *Inc.,* 1984, (Jan.), pp. 42–52.

Roberts, N. C. "Transforming Leadership: Sources, Process, Consequences." Paper presented at the annual meeting of the Academy of Management, Boston, 1984.

Rokeach, M. *Beliefs, Attitudes, and Values.* San Francisco: Jossey-Bass, 1968.

Rothenburg, A. *The Emerging Goddess.* Chicago: University of Chicago Press, 1979.

Rubin, Z. *Liking and Loving: An Invitation to Social Psychology.* New York: Holt, Rinehart & Winston, 1973.

Salancik, G., and Meindle, J. "Corporate Attributions as Management Illusion of Control." *Administrative Science Quarterly,* 1984, *29,* 238–254.

Sashkin, M. "The Visionary Leader." In J. A. Conger, R. N. Kanungo, and Associates (eds.), *Charismatic Leadership.* San Francisco: Jossey-Bass, 1988.

Schein, E. H. *Organizational Culture and Leadership.* San Francisco: Jossey-Bass, 1985.

Schlenker, B. R. *Impression Management.* Monterey: Brooks/Cole, 1980.

Schwenk, C. R. "Information, Cognitive Biases, and Commitment to a Course of Action." *Academy of Management Review,* 1986, *11* (2), 298–310.

Sculley, J. "Corporate Antihero: John Sculley." *Inc.,* Oct. 1987a, pp. 49–59.

Sculley, J. "Sculley's Lessons from Inside Apple." *Fortune,* Sept. 14, 1987b, *116,* 108–111.

Selznick, P. *Leadership in Administration.* New York: Harper & Row, 1957.

Shamir, B., House, R. J., and Arthur, M. B. "The Transformational Effects of Charismatic Leadership—A Motivational Theory." Working paper. Boston: Suffolk University, 1988.

Shaver, K. G. *An Introduction to Attribution Processes.* Cambridge, Mass.: Winthrop Publishers, 1975.

Sigel, E. "Is Home Banking for Real?" *Datamation,* Sept. 15, 1986, *32,* 128–134.

Simon, H. A. "Information Processing Models of Cognition." *Annual Review of Psychology,* 1979, *30,* 363.

Smith, B. J. "An Initial Test of a Theory of Charismatic Leadership Based on the Responses of Subordinates." Unpublished doctoral dissertation, University of Toronto, 1982.

Snow, D. A., Rochford, E. B., Worden, S. K., and Benford, R. D. "Frame Alignment Processes, Micromobilization, and Movement Participation." *American Sociological Review,* Aug. 1986, *51,* 464–481.

Starbuck, W. H., Greve, A., and Hedberg, B. "Responding to Crises." *Journal of Business Administration,* 1978, *9,* 111–137.

Staw, B. M. "Knee Deep in the Big Muddy: A Study of Escalating Commitment to a Chosen Course of Action." *Organizational Behavior and Human Performance,* 1976, *16,* 27–44.

Staw, B. M. "The Escalation of Commitment to a Course of Action." *Academy of Management Review,* 1981, *6,* 577–587.

Staw, B. M., and Ross, J. "Commitment to a Policy Decision: A Multi-Theoretical Perspective." *Administrative Science Quarterly,* 1978, *23,* 40–64.

Stengrevics, J. "Mary Kay Cosmetics." Boston: Harvard Business School, 1981.

Taylor, A. "Iacocca's Time of Trouble." *Fortune,* Mar. 14, 1988, pp. 79–88.

Tichy, N. M., and Devanna, M. A. *The Transformational Leader.* New York: Wiley, 1986.

Trice, H. M., and Beyer, J. M. "Charisma and Its Routinization in Two Social Movement Organizations." In L. Cummings and B. Staw (eds.), *Research in Organizational Behavior.* Vol. 8. Greenwich, Conn.: JAI Press, 1986.

Tucker, R. B. "Federal Express's Fred Smith." *Inc.,* 1986 (Oct.), pp. 35–50.

Tucker, R. C. "The Theory of Charismatic Leadership." In D. A. Rustow (ed.), *Philosophers and Kings.* New York: George Braziller, 1970.

Tunley, R. "Mary Kay's Sweet Smell of Success." *Reader's Digest,* Nov. 1978, p. 5.

Tushman, M. L., and Romanelli, E. "Organizational Evolution: A Metamorphosis Model of Convergence and Reorientation." In L. Cummings and B. Staw (eds.), *Research in Organizational Behavior.* Vol. 7. Greenwich, Conn.: JAI Press, 1985.

Tushman, M. L., Virany, B., and Romanelli, E. "Effects of CEO and Executive Team Succession: A Longitudinal Analysis." Working paper. New York: Graduate School of Business, Columbia University, 1987.

Uttal, B. "The Adventures of Steven Jobs (Cont'd)." *Fortune,* Oct. 14, 1985a, pp. 119–121.

Uttal, B. "Behind the Fall of Steve Jobs." *Fortune,* Aug. 5, 1985b, pp. 20–24.

Walster, E., Aronson, D., and Abrahams, D. "On Increasing the Persuasiveness of a Low Prestige Communicator." *Journal of Experimental Social Psychology,* 1966, *2,* 325–342.

Weber, M. *The Theory of Social and Economic Organization.* (A. M. Henderson and T. Parsons, trans.; T. Parsons, ed.) New York: Free Press, 1947. (Originally published 1924.)

Wensberg, P. C. *Land's Polaroid.* Boston: Houghton Mifflin, 1987.

Westley, F. R., and Bird, F. B. "The Social Psychology of Organizational Commitment: A Critical Review of Classical Theories." Working paper. Montreal: McGill University, 1988.

Westley, F., and Mintzberg, H. "Profiles of Strategic Vision: Levesque and Iacocca." In J. A. Conger, R. N. Kanungo, and Associates (eds.), *Charismatic Leadership.* San Francisco: Jossey-Bass, 1988.

White, J. A. "AT&T's McGill Expected to Quit as Head of Unregulated Business Product Unit." *Wall Street Journal,* June 7, 1983, p. 4.

Whitestone, D. *People Express.* Boston: Harvard Business School, 1983.

Wilbins, R. "Learning to Tack." *Bell Telephone Magazine,* 1982, *5,* 14–16.

Wilkins, A. "Organizational Stories as an Expression of Management Philosophy: Implications for Social Control in Organizations." Unpublished doctoral dissertation, Stanford University, 1979.

Willner, A. R. *The Spellbinders: Charismatic Political Leadership.* New Haven: Yale University Press, 1984.

Wright, J. P. *On a Clear Day You Can See General Motors.* New York: Avon Books, 1979.

Yukl, G. A. *Leadership in Organizations.* Englewood Cliffs, N.J.: Prentice-Hall, 1989.

Yukl, G. A., and Van Fleet, D. D. "Cross-Situational Multi-Method Research on Military Leader Effectiveness." *Organizational Behavior and Human Performance,* 1982, *30,* 87–108.

Zaleznik, A., and Kets de Vries, M.F.R. *Power and the Corporate Mind.* Boston: Houghton Mifflin, 1975.

Zinn, L. "Home Banking Is Here—If You Want It." *Business Week,* Feb. 29, 1988, pp. 108–109.

INDEX

205